WORLD HISTORY SERIES ■ ■ ■

The Relocation of the North American Indian

by
John M. Dunn

Lucent Books, P.O. Box 289011, San Diego, CA 92198-9011

Titles in the World History Series

The Age of Feudalism
Ancient Greece
The Cuban Revolution
The Early Middle Ages
Elizabethan England
The End of the Cold War
The French and Indian War
The French Revolution
Greek and Roman Theater
Hitler's Reich

The Hundred Years' War
The Inquisition
Modern Japan
The Relocation of the
    North American Indian
The Roman Empire
The Roman Republic
The Russian Revolution
Traditional Japan
The Travels of Marco Polo

Library of Congress Cataloging-in-Publication Data

Dunn, John M., 1949-
    The relocation of the North American Indian / by John
M. Dunn.
        p. cm. — (World history series)
    Includes bibliographical references and index.
    ISBN 1-56006-240-1 (acid free)
    1. Indians of North America—Relocation. 2. Indians of
North America—Land Tenure. 3. Indians of North America—
Reservations.
I. Title. II. Series.
E93.D86 1995
970.004'97—dc20   94-3623
                                                          CIP
                                                           AC

Contents

Foreword   4
Important Dates in the History of the Relocation
    of the North American Indian   6

INTRODUCTION
A Conscience-Stained Past   8

CHAPTER 1
Whose Lands?   10

CHAPTER 2
Pushing the Indians West   23

CHAPTER 3
Pushed to the Mississippi   34

CHAPTER 4
Forced Removal Begins   46

CHAPTER 5
The Disappearing Frontier   59

CHAPTER 6
Revolts, Removals, and Reservations   70

CHAPTER 7
The Final Stand   81

CHAPTER 8
Trying to Make Indians White   92

CHAPTER 9
Forced into the Twentieth Century   102

EPILOGUE:
Confronting the Present   112

Notes   115
For Further Reading   119
Additional Works Consulted   120
Index   124
Picture Credits   128
About the Author   128

Foreword

Each year on the first day of school, nearly every history teacher faces the task of explaining why his or her students should study history. One logical answer to this question is that exploring what happened in our past explains how the things we often take for granted—our customs, ideas, and institutions—came to be. As statesman and historian Winston Churchill put it, "Every nation or group of nations has its own tale to tell. Knowledge of the trials and struggles is necessary to all who would comprehend the problems, perils, challenges, and opportunities which confront us today." Thus, a study of history puts modern ideas and institutions in perspective. For example, though the founders of the United States were talented and creative thinkers, they clearly did not invent the concept of democracy. Instead, they adapted some democratic ideas that had originated in ancient Greece and with which the Romans, the British, and others had experimented. An exploration of these cultures, then, reveals their very real connection to us through institutions that continue to shape our daily lives.

Another reason often given for studying history is the idea that lessons exist in the past from which contemporary societies can benefit and learn. This idea, although controversial, has always been an intriguing one for historians. Those that agree that society can benefit from the past often quote philosopher George Santayana's famous statement, "Those who cannot remember the past are condemned to repeat it." Historians who ascribe to Santayana's philosophy believe that, for example, studying the events that led up to the major world wars or other significant historical events would allow society to chart a different and more favorable course in the future.

Just as difficult as convincing students to realize the importance of studying history is the search for useful and interesting supplementary materials that present historical events in a context that can be easily understood. The volumes in Lucent Books' World History Series attempt to present a broad, balanced, and penetrating view of the march of history. Ancient Egypt's important wars and rulers, for example, are presented against the rich and colorful backdrop of Egyptian religious, social, and cultural developments. The series engages the reader by enhancing historical events with these cultural contexts. For example, in *Ancient Greece*, the text covers the role of women in that society. Slavery is discussed in *The Roman Empire*, as well as how slaves earned their freedom. The numerous and varied aspects of everyday life in these and other societies are explored in each volume of the series. Additionally, the series covers the major political, cultural, and philosophical ideas as the torch of civilization is passed from ancient Mesopotamia and Egypt, through Greece, Rome, Medieval Europe, and other world cultures, to the modern day.

The material in the series is formatted in a thorough, precise, and organized manner. Each volume offers the reader a comprehensive and clearly written overview of an important historical event or period. The topic under discussion is placed in a broad, historical context. For example, *The Italian Renaissance* begins with a discussion of the High Middle Ages and the loss of central control that allowed certain Italian cities to develop artistically. The book ends by looking forward to the Reformation and interpreting the societal changes that grew out of the Renaissance. Thus, students are not only involved in an historical era, but also enveloped by the events leading up to that era and the events following it.

One important and unique feature in the World History Series is the primary and secondary source quotations that richly supplement each volume. These quotes are useful in a number of ways. First, they allow students access to sources they would not normally be exposed to because of the difficulty and obscurity of the original source. The quotations range from interesting anecdotes to far-sighted cultural perspectives and are drawn from historical witnesses both past and present. Second, the quotes demonstrate how and where historians themselves derive their information on the past as they strive to reach a consensus on historical events. Lastly, all of the quotes are footnoted, familiarizing students with the citation process and allowing them to verify quotes and/or look up the original source if the quote piques their interest.

Finally, the books in the World History Series provide a detailed launching point for further research. Each book contains a bibliography specifically geared toward student research. A second, annotated bibliography introduces students to all the sources the author consulted when compiling the book. A chronology of important dates gives students an overview, at a glance, of the topic covered. Where applicable, a glossary of terms is included.

In short, the series is designed not only to acquaint readers with the basics of history, but also to make them aware that their lives are a part of an ongoing human saga. Perhaps they will then come to the same realization as famed historian Arnold Toynbee. In his monumental work, *A Study of History*, he wrote about becoming aware of history flowing through him in a mighty current, and of his own life "welling like a wave in the flow of this vast tide."

Important Dates in the History of the Relocation of the North American Indian

1622	1650	1675	1700	1725	1750	1775	1800

1622–1646
English defeat Powhatans in Virginia, confiscate their lands, and round them up in first reservations

1636–1637
Pequot War: Puritans kill 600 Pequots and take Indian lands

1676
End of King Philip's War; after nineteen years, Wampanoag tribe is defeated and sold into slavery, loses lands to whites

1754–1763
England defeats France in French and Indian War; England dominates North America east of Mississippi

1763
Pontiac's three-year rebellion begins; Proclamation of 1763 sets Indian border along Appalachian Mountains

1768–1770
Delawares sign first land treaty with Continental Congress; Indians and whites parley at Fort Stanwix, New York, Hard Labor, and Lochaber in West Virginia, and push Proclamation line farther west

1776
American Revolution begins; Indian support is divided between colonies and England

1783
Lands west of Appalachian Mountains open to migration

1787
Northwest Ordinance spells out arrangements for organized white settlement in the Great Lakes area

1790–1794
Little Turtle's War; Treaty of Greenville; Indians cede parts of Ohio and Indiana

1803
The Louisiana Purchase opens one-third of North America to westward expansion and offers a place for removed tribes; Jefferson begins relocation policy

1809–1811
Tecumseh's confederacy is smashed; Indian resistance to removal is very greatly weakened

1810
William Henry Harrison, in process of negotiating fifteen treaties, requires Indians to cede land that now forms parts of Ohio, Indiana, Illinois, Wisconsin, and Michigan

1814
Jackson's troops defeat Creeks, who are forced to cede eastern Alabama

1823
Seminoles cede most of West Florida

1824
U.S. Bureau of Indian Affairs is created

1830–1839
U.S. Indian Removal Act forces the Five Civilized Tribes, as well as other tribes, to move to Indian Territory

1833
Glowing reports of Oregon region entice migration to the Far West, leading to displacement of Native Americans living there

1834
Lands are defined in new Indian Territory; Black Hawk War results in forced relocation of all tribes in Northwest to Indian Territory

1835–1843
Osceola leads Seminole uprising; Indians lose most of Florida to whites

1848
Defeated in war, Mexico cedes California, Arizona, Texas, New Mexico, Utah, and Nevada to United States; whites encroach on Indian lands in these areas

1851
Fort Laramie Conference; United States promises annuities to tribes that allow settlers to pass through to Far West; peace is short-lived as settlers multiply and stake claims in Indian territories

1854
Indian Territory is squeezed by emigrants from mining communities from Far West and from populated East; Nebraska is split into two territories; United States encourages settlement into each; new round of treaties opens nearby Indian lands to settlers

1859
California Gold Rush entices flood of white settlers to the Pacific coast; Osage tribe is forced off lands at gunpoint

1861
Civil War begins, temporarily easing pressure on Indian lands; Arapahos agree to U.S. treaty giving away lands in present-day Nebraska, Kansas, Colorado, and Wyoming

1862
Sioux uprisings end in forced land cessions in Minnesota

1825	1850	1875	1900	1925	1950	1975	1995

1863–1868
Navajos, defeated in war, cede lands in Rio Grande valley, make forced march to join Mescalero Apaches on Bosque Redondo reservation

1864
Chivington Massacre at Sand Creek; Arapaho and Cheyenne war in Colorado

1865
Five Civilized Tribes lose half of Indian Territory as punishment for supporting the South in the Civil War

1867–1868
U.S. Peace Commission relocates western tribes on two main reservations on Five Civilized Tribes lands; Plains tribes cede lands along Arkansas and Canadian Rivers; Sherman called in to command attacks on rebelling "non-treaty" Indians; Sioux give up lands in Wyoming and Montana

1868
Custer leads massacre of Cheyenne on Washita River

1869–1874
Indian wars in the West; 200 Indian battles

1871
Congress ceases to recognize Indian tribes as nations

1874
Gold rush in Black Hills triggers white invasion of Sioux lands

1876
July 5, Custer and 264 soldiers die at Little Big Horn; American nation is aroused

1877
After having ceded lands in Idaho

and Oregon, Chief Joseph and Nez Percé make unsuccessful attempt to escape to Canada

1881
Helen Hunt Jackson's *A Century of Dishonor* is published

1885
Major Crimes Act passed; federal government, not tribes, now metes out penalties for felonies on reservations

1887
Dawes Severalty (General Allotment) Act divides reservation lands to Indians on individual rather than tribal basis; surplus land sold to whites

1889–1895
Series of Oklahoma "land runs" open; lands on Indian Territory given to white homesteaders

1890
U.S. Army massacres Sioux at Wounded Knee, South Dakota, in last major act of violence in U.S.-Indian wars

1897
President William McKinley announces Indian Territory to become part of United States

1903
Lone Wolf loses legal bid to stop treaty violation

1906
United States takes sacred Taos lands in New Mexico

1907
Oklahoma and Indian Territory become forty-sixth state

1924
Snyder Act grants Native Americans U.S. citizenship and the right to vote

1934
Two-thirds of Indian reservation lands now gone since 1887; John Collier becomes Commissioner of Indian Affairs; President Franklin D. Roosevelt's Indian Reorganization Act ends allotment and creates new policy of self-determination for Indians, returning surplus land to Indians

1945
Collier resigns; termination idea gains popularity

1946
Indian Claims Commission is set up

1954–1962
Termination is in effect; 109 Indian groups are terminated

1958–1960s
Termination ends

1961
Indian conference in Chicago produces Declaration of Indian Purpose; rising Indian militancy

1970
Nixon policies grant more self-determination to reservations; sacred lands returned to Taos

1973
Sioux militants take over town of Wounded Knee and confront armed authorities

1980s–present
Repeated attempts by government agencies to open Indian lands for mining, skiing, or other forms of development

A Conscience-Stained Past

When Europeans arrived in the New World, they found a vast variety of native people who ranged across the continent of North America. These people comprised more than three hundred separate tribes whose members spoke nearly as many languages. The largest concentrations lived along the Pacific coast, in the Southwest, and in the woodlands east of the Mississippi River.

Individual North American Indian tribes differed vastly from one another. Some tribes were composed of nomadic hunters. Other tribes, like the Cherokee and Creek in the Southeast, were sedentary farmers. The Hopi and Zuni of the Southwest dwelled in adobe homes built into the sides of steep canyon walls. Some tribes lived peacefully with their neighbors, while others were warrior tribes who raided their neighbors as a way of life. Blood feuds and warfare among North American tribes, in fact, were common long before whites arrived in the New World.

A vast variety of Native American tribes populated the New World before the arrival of Europeans. Unfortunately, lack of intertribal unity and cooperation would allow Europeans to easily dominate and conquer Indians.

Indians attack white settlers. Native Americans believed that their opposition to whites was self-defense.

Despite their many differences, the Indians of North America had much in common. They tended to live in bands, tribes, and confederations. Men and women usually married and raised their own children. Tribal elders generally served as advisers, not dictators. Most Native Americans believed in the supernatural, especially in a universal god, the Great Spirit.

At first, many of the first white settlers and Indians tried to live in peace. Soon, though, whites and Indians began to fight. Some of the time, people on each side fought in self-defense. On other occasions, fear and revenge motivated the bloodletting. All too often, Native Americans and whites alike systematically and unnecessarily killed unarmed women and children.

The inevitable outcome of these encounters was the steady removal and dispossession of Indians from their native lands. It was a process that lasted four hundred years and ended with Native Americans confined to an area equal to 2.3 percent of the continent.

On the surface, the history of the removal of the American Indian is a tale of conquest, of white Europeans driving American Indians from their native soil and annihilating their ancient cultures. But on a deeper level, as author S. M. Barrett suggests, the struggle between Europeans and Native Americans was largely a cultural clash. Differing concepts of religion and ethics, different languages, and differences in food, medicine, dress, societal customs, punishment, justice, medical care, leadership, time, and land possession probably made armed conflict unavoidable.

Only a few million Indians dwelled in the Americas when white explorers first appeared. To Europeans this meant that most of the continent was almost uninhabited, and thus available to anyone. And this perception led perhaps to the greatest clash of all—the bloody struggle over who would have the land.

Chapter

1 Whose Lands?

Who owned the vast unsettled stretches of North America? This question lies at the core of the clash of Indian and European cultures. Even today, as in the past, many Native Americans view the European conquest of North America as property theft. "[During the past five hundred years], . . . we have been denied our way of life, our expression of faith, and the lands on which we have lived for thousands of years," writes Indian historian Little Rock Reed.[1]

But exactly which lands belonged to Indians? Lands they physically occupied? The lands they hunted on? And what rightful claim did they have to the vast sections of uninhabited territory? In 1898 Theodore Roosevelt, who later became president of the United States, summed up a prevalent white attitude concerning these questions: "The white settler has merely moved into an uninhabited waste; he does not feel that he is committing a wrong, for he knows perfectly well that the land is really owned by no one."[2]

All but Invisible

Historian Peter H. Wood, however, argues that whites greatly underestimated the number of Indians who originally lived on the American continent, to justify taking their lands. Many textbooks, Wood writes,

> have included maps of the "peopling" or "settling" of . . . supposedly "virgin" land. They showed a small parade of colored dots, representing European immigrants, moving westward across an otherwise blank continent. The [Native] Americans who already lived here have remained all but invisible to later generations.[3]

Even from the very first encounters between natives and Europeans, Europeans arrogantly denied or ignored the right of Native Americans to the land they occupied. One of Christopher Columbus's first official acts upon arriving in the New World in 1492 was to claim possession of an inhabited island in the Caribbean. "I ordered the captains of the Pinta and Nina," Columbus wrote in his journal on October 12, 1492, "to bear faith and witness that I was taking possession of this island for the King and Queen [of Spain]."[4]

Furthermore, he noted, "My desire was not to pass any island without taking possession, so that, one having been taken, the same may be said of all."[5]

What convinced Columbus that he had the right to claim these lands? Like many other Europeans of the fifteenth century, he believed the "act of discovery" alone gave him such authority. This concept was so powerful among whites, in fact, that as late as 1823 U.S. Supreme Court chief justice John Marshall ruled in a land dispute case that the act of discovery gave ultimate title to lands in the New World to the Europeans.

In 1493 Columbus's acts received further legitimacy when Pope Alexander IV, the head of the Catholic Church, assumed the right to grant to whomever he pleased sovereignty of any new lands not already possessed by a Christian ruler. According to Catholic Church doctrine: "The Pope . . . has power not only over Christians, but also over all infidels [non-Christians]."[6] Columbus's discovery of new lands, therefore, increased the territory over which the pope could cast his authority.

In 1494 the pope exercised this power by declaring the so-called line of demarcation, dividing the New World between Spain and Portugal, to avoid territorial disputes between the two Catholic countries. Portugal received the portion of South America now known as Brazil; the rest of the New World went to Spain.

And what if the original inhabitants objected to the confiscation of their lands by a European country, such as Spain? Author Alistair Cooke explains:

> If . . . a kingdom or a tribe was hostile, it was no more than a Christian duty to suppress it, to topple its idols, and raise the Cross on the grounds that the natives were double traitors; to the Pope of Rome and the King [of the colonizing country] . . . two . . . [gods] of whom they had never heard.[7]

Christopher Columbus greets the inhabitants of the New World as he claims the land in the name of Spain. Such attitudes of land ownership would lead to inevitable clashes with the natives.

Creating New Spain

Not long after Columbus's first voyage to America, Spain dispatched other adventurers to the New World to obtain gold, silver, slaves, and agricultural products from the lands claimed for the Spanish crown. Spanish authorities also granted land titles to Spaniards willing to start settlements and colonies.

Officially the Spanish government and the Catholic Church forbade the mistreatment of the aboriginal peoples the colonists encountered. However, the men called conquistadors, who sought fame and riches, often treated Native Americans with extreme brutality. They justified this brutality by viewing Indian cultural practices with contempt. In the Caribbean countries, native religious practices often included cannibalism, human sacrifice, and the impersonation of animals in costume and dance. Witnessing such unfamiliar rituals convinced the Spanish that those who performed them were subhuman devils and enemies of Christianity who deserved condemnation and horrendous punishments.

Compensating for their lack of sophisticated weaponry, Native Americans disguise themselves with deer hides to get close enough to kill deer with bows and arrows. Such practices seemed primitive and strange to white Europeans.

Throughout the Americas, the Spanish conquistadors left a dark legacy of enslavement, torture, and murder. They stole Indian riches, burned villages, and confiscated land. By using such methods, Spain created an empire in the New World that ranged from South America to Florida to California.

Europeans Compete for Indian Lands

Along with the Spanish and Portuguese, other European nations—Sweden, Denmark, Holland, France, Russia, and England—arrived in the New World with territorial plans of their own.

Though these nations generally ignored the pope's line of demarcation, they did share the conviction that discovery gave "sovereignty of the soil." At the same time, most Europeans also recognized that Native Americans had a "right of occupancy" to the lands they lived on. The Europeans insisted, however, that this right was "alienable," or transferable to others. And to the European way of thinking, this transfer of occupancy rights could take place either by purchase or by conquest—and whites were eager to employ both means.

The French Stake a Claim

In 1608 French ships arrived on the northeast coast of the North American continent. "In the name of . . . Louis the Great . . . King of France . . . I . . . do now take . . . this country of Louisiana," declared the French explorer La Salle.[8]

La Salle proclaims Louisiana a territory of France. The French got along well with the Indians because they wanted to use land to hunt and fish, not for settlement.

After establishing Quebec in New France (Canada) as their main colony, the French expanded southward along the Mississippi River.

Unlike many other explorers from across the Atlantic, the French treated Indians humanely and fairly. Less interested than other Europeans in land rights, the French sought Indian help in developing a lucrative fur trade in the New World. French trappers blended in with Indian tribes and learned their languages and customs. The French also hoped that Indian

The Pilgrims land in North America. The Pilgrims' lack of respect for Indian culture and claim to land led to cruel attacks on both sides.

warriors from the northeastern tribes such as the Abenaki, Algonquin, and Huron would help them in repelling France's traditional enemy, the English, who were also in North America seeking new lands.

The English Settlers

The English began systematically pushing Indians off their native lands. The process began at England's first permanent colony at Jamestown, Virginia, in 1606 on land that was "chartered"—or officially lent—to settlers by King James. A new form of business organization called a joint-stock company provided the financial backing for each overseas colony. Under this system, investors pooled together all their capital, or investment money, and shared the profits and losses of the colony.

The English settlers' specific goals were to trade with Indians, to find a passageway through the American continent to China for purposes of trade, and to locate mineral wealth.

From the time of their arrival, the settlers had trouble with Indians: a roving band wounded seventeen Britons and killed a boy. Although relations with the neighboring Powhatan tribe initially were quite peaceful, the English came to fear and despise the Indians. Shocked by the appearance of the Powhatans, many whites considered the native people to be savages, if not devils. Wrote Jamestown leader Capt. John Smith of local Indians in 1609:

Their women some have their legs, hands, breasts and faces cunningly embroidered with diverse works, as beasts, serpents, artificially wrought into their flesh with black spots. In each ear commonly they have three great holes where at they hang chains, bracelets, or copper. Some of their men wear in those holes a small green and yellow colored snake, near half a yard in length, which crawling and lapping herself about his neck often times familiarly would kiss his lips. Others wear a dead rat tied by the tail.[9]

The Powhatans equally feared and distrusted the heavily armed white newcomers.

"I am informed that you wish to conquer more than to trade," Chief Wahunsonacock told John Smith. "[Y]ou know my people must be afraid to come near you with their corn, so long as you go armed with such a retinue [group of attendants]."[10]

In 1622 hostilities broke out when servants of a Jamestown planter killed an important Indian leader to avenge the death of their master in an earlier incident. In return, Powhatans killed 347 settlers in a few hours.

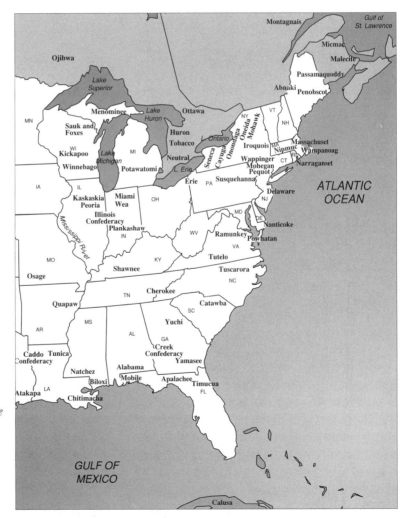

This map shows the locations of North American tribes in the eastern part of North America at the time of European arrival. The close proximity of Native American tribes to European settlements led to inevitable conflict.

Bay Colony governor John Winthrop took a typical European attitude toward Native Americans when he claimed Europeans had more of a right to the land because Indians had done little to develop it.

The English retaliated by trying to exterminate the Powhatans. "It is infinitely better to have no heathen among us, who were but thorns in our sides, than to be at peace and league with them," declared Francis Wyatt, the governor of the Virginia settlement.[11]

The English decided to use any means necessary to destroy their enemy, including trickery and deceit. Governor Wyatt, for example, once invited Indian leader Openchancanough and his warriors to a "peace conference" to settle their differences. At this gathering, whites served the unsuspecting Indians poisoned food, and pounced on and killed many of the two hundred who fell sick.

Officials of the London company that provided financial backing for Jamestown complained upon learning of Wyatt's actions. They feared that bloodshed would lead to instability and bad long-term relations with the Indians, which would hamper future colonial efforts. In answer to their qualms, however, the company officials received this unapologetic reply from the Virginia Council of State:

> Wee hold nothing iniuste [unjust] . . . that may tend to their [the Indians'] ruine. . . . Stratagems were ever allowed against all enemies, but with these neither fayre Warr nor good quarter is ever to be held, nor is their other hope of their subervisione, who every may inform you to the contrarie.[12]

The Jamestown settlers defeated the Indians in 1646, confiscated their lands, and forced survivors to live in constricted areas. This roundup of Native Americans foreshadowed the pattern that would be used by whites to control Indians for the next three hundred years. In 1656 Virginia and the United Colonies jointly developed the idea of setting up certain areas for "exclusive Indian use," thus giving birth to the idea of Indian reservations.

Problems to the North

Relations between whites and Indians had already turned sour at the Massachusetts Bay Colony when Puritan settlers began to encroach on Indian lands. Although Virginia had been the original destination of the Puritans, strong winds blew them far off course, and when they landed at Plymouth Rock in 1620, they decided to stay in the Northeast. Thus, these immigrants had no legal basis for settling where they did. As George Manypenny, commissioner of Indian Affairs in the 1850s, wrote:

> Before they left home they had permission from . . . [their king] to go out and settle in the wilderness, and they did not appear to have any scruple about taking possession of the country where they landed, although it was not within the limits of the Virginia Colony.[13]

In 1625 some of the newcomers asked Samoset, a local chief of the Wampanoags, to give them twelve thousand acres of land. The request amused the Indian leader who, like many other Native Americans, believed that land was boundless, not to be owned by anyone. "To humor these strangers in their strange ways," writes historian Dee Brown, "[Samoset] went through a ceremony of transferring the land and made his mark on a paper for them. It was the first deed of Indian land to English colonists."[14]

But amusement turned to anger and hostility when more settlers arrived and took land without asking. And when Indians objected to the ceaseless clearing of forests and the building of houses and other buildings, the Bay Colony's governor, John Winthrop, responded that colonists were merely filling a "vacuum" in the wilderness. Besides, he said, Indians had not tamed the lands they lived on and therefore had no legal right to them.

The Puritans Take Indian Lands

In 1630 an even larger number of Puritans arrived. Their goal: to build a society based on their religious convictions.

To build permanent settlements, the Puritans needed land. They said they were willing to pay for any cultivated land they took from Indians, but they considered undeveloped wildlands free for the taking to anyone. Whenever Indians tried to prevent seizure of lands, wild or otherwise, the Puritans consulted their Bibles. According to historian Howard Zinn:

> The Puritans . . . appealed to the Bible: Psalms 2:8: "Ask of me, and I shall give thee the heathen for thine inheritance, and the uttermost parts of the earth for thy possession."
>
> And to justify their use of force to take the land, they cited Romans 13:2: "Whosoever therefore resisteth the power, resisteth the ordinance of God: and they that resist shall receive to themselves damnation."[15]

The Puritans believed that they possessed a God-given right to use violence against Indians and to take Indian lands. And like the Spaniards before them, they defined their encounters with Indians in religious terms. The wilderness was not merely uncultivated land; it was the wild land of devils. Many English firmly believed that Satan had brought Indians to untamed America, which he saw as a last refuge in the world to escape the advance of Christianity. Thus, many Puritans saw Indians as agents of the devil whose purpose was to tempt and destroy the settlers.

Fear of Indian devils was so powerful, writes author Gary Wills, that Puritans thought "[e]ven friendly overtures [from Indians] were likely to be part of a larger strategy to disarm Christians."[16]

Bay Colony War

Tensions between Indians and English settlers in Massachusetts exploded into warfare in 1637 when Indians killed an English sea captain who had kidnapped members of the Pequot tribe and tried to sell them as slaves. During a surprise retaliatory raid against the Indians on May 26, English colonists slaughtered men, women, and children and burned wigwams while many slept inside.

"It is supposed that no less than five or six hundred Pequod souls were brought down to hell that day," wrote Puritan minister, Cotton Mather.[17]

The victorious whites thereafter enjoyed peace until 1657, when a Wampanoag leader named Metacomet, whom

---

King Powhatan's Warning

In 1609 Capt. John Smith of Jamestown recorded these words of Wahunsonacock, or King Powhatan. The complaint of the leader of the Powhatan Confederacy—over mistreatment from whites that later led to war—is found in Native American Testimony: An Anthology of Indian and White Relations, First Encounter to Dispossession, *edited by Peter Nabokov.*

"Why should you [the English] take by force that from us which you can have by love? Why should you destroy us, who have provided you with food? What can you get by war? We can hide our provisions, and fly into the woods; and then you must consequently famish by wronging your friends [the Indians]. What is the cause of your jealousy? You see us unarmed, and willing to supply your wants, if you will come in a friendly manner, and not with swords and guns, as to invade an enemy.

I am not so simple, as not to know it is better to eat good meat, lie well, and sleep quietly with my women and children; to laugh and be merry with the English; and, being their friend, to have copper, hatchets, and whatever else I want, than to fly from all, to lie cold in the woods, feed upon acorns, roots, and such trash, and to be so hunted, that I cannot rest, eat, or sleep. In such circumstances, my men must watch, and if a twig should but break, all would cry out, 'Here come Captain Smith'; and so, in this miserable manner, to end my miserable life; and, Captain Smith, this might be soon your fate too, through your rashness and unadvisedness [bad judgment].

I, therefore, exhort you to peaceable councils; and, above all, I insist that the guns and swords, the cause of all our jealousy and uneasiness, be removed and sent away."

Wampanoag leader Metacomet, called King Philip by whites, united several neighboring tribes and led an uprising against white settlers.

the settlers called King Philip, forged an alliance between the Wampanoag and the Narraganset and Nipmuc tribes, to halt the English advance on Indian lands.

The alliance caused many whites to panic. They feared that the Indians would go on a rampage of revenge, scalping, murdering, raping, and torturing.

In February 1675, Mary Rowlandson, a New England mother and wife, saw these fears turn into reality when Indians attacked Lancaster, Massachusetts. She later wrote:

> Now is the dreadful hour come that I have often heard of. . . . Some in our house were fighting for their lives.

Others wallowing in their blood, the house on fire over our heads, and the bloody heathen ready to knock us on the head if we stirred out.[18]

Of the thirty-seven whites in the besieged house, Indians killed twelve and took the remaining captives, including Mary Rowlandson and her wounded six-year-old child, who later died.

The fighting continued for years, as King Philip and his united warriors kept attacking white settlements. The attacks finally came to an end one night in August 1676, when Massachusetts and Connecticut troops tracked Philip down in a swamp, where he was shot by an Indian ally of the whites. Soldiers then quartered the Indian leader, severed his head, and placed it in the Fort Hill Tower, where it remained for twenty-five years, its eye sockets serving as nests for birds, symbolizing broken Indian power.

The victorious colonists then severely punished survivors. Many Wampanoags, including Philip's wife and young children, were sold into slavery in the West Indies, and others were forced to move onto nearby farms owned and run by white overseers.

King Philip's uprising created such widespread fear and hate throughout New England that many colonists turned against all Indians. Even friendly allies, such as the Mohegan and the Pequot, were forced off their lands.

A Pattern of War and Removal

There were numerous brutal and bloody conflicts between the English and the

European settlers clear land to establish a homestead. Encouraged by England to settle North America, such settlers unwittingly forced natives to relocate or fight to regain their land.

Indians along the eastern seaboard from Georgia to New England during the 1600s. Inevitably, the outcome of the fighting was the same: The Indians were subdued, annihilated, enslaved, or driven away, as English settlers occupied their lands and moved ever inland, following rivers and relentlessly "taming" and settling new lands. Many English began to argue that by right of discovery all North America belonged to the English king; and only the king, not Indians, could grant land titles.

In London, however, government officials disapproved of the growing use of violence by land-seeking settlers. In an attempt to prevent more bloodshed and to placate Indians, the officials developed a new colonial policy that required Britons to recognize the Indians' right of occupancy

and the need to compensate the native people for any land that was taken.

The New World settlers, however, lived far from English authority and generally did as they pleased.

English Advances

As English settlers relentlessly encroached on and confiscated Indian lands, they tried to justify their actions with a host of philosophical reasons. In the seventeenth century, many Europeans believed that certain "natural laws" governed human affairs and were similar to those that controlled physical phenomena. One of these natural laws dealt with land use. Some European philosophers argued that land was intended by God to be used properly by humans. That is, those who were willing to make the best use of land had a "natural right" to take possession of it. According to this argument, a group of people such as the American Indians, who relied primarily on hunting for their sustenance, was not using the land wisely, because hunting requires vast stretches of land to provide enough game for food. Therefore, nomadic Indians had no "right of occupancy" to wilderness areas because they never stayed long in one place. Only by farming, insisted the Europeans, could land be used efficiently and productively, as God intended. This point of view was expressed by an eighteenth-century Swiss jurist, Emmerich von Vattel:

> The people of Europe, too closely pent up at home, finding land [in the New World] of which the savages stood in no particular need, and of which they made no actual and constant use, were lawfully entitled to take possession of it, and settle it with colonies. . . . The savages of North America had no right to appropriate all that vast continent to themselves.[19]

The English, like many other Europeans, also agreed with English philosopher John Locke, who asserted that humans had

---

Indians Have No Right to Land?

Theodore Roosevelt, the twenty-sixth president of the United States, was also a prolific writer and spent much time in the West. This excerpt from his book The Winning of the West, *published in 1889, as the final wars between the United States and Indians drew to a close, appears in* Christopher Columbus and His Legacy, *edited by Mary Ellen Jones.*

"The Indian had no ownership of the land in the way in which we understand the term. The tribes lived far apart; each had for its hunting-grounds all the territory from which it was not barred by rivals. Each looked with jealousy upon all interlopers, but each was prompt to act as an interloper when occasion offered. Every good hunting-ground was claimed by many [Indian] nations. It was rare, indeed, that any tribe had an uncontested title to a large tract of land; where such title existed, it rested, not on actual occupancy and cultivation, but on the recent butchery of weaker rivals. For instance, there were a dozen tribes, all of whom hunted in Kentucky, and fought each other there, all of whom had equally good titles to the soil, and not one of whom acknowledged the right of any other; as a matter of fact they had therein no right, save the right of the strongest. The land no more belonged to them than it belonged to [Daniel] Boone and the white hunters who first visited it."

a natural right to "life, liberty, and property." And to the Europeans, land was indeed property—something that could be owned, bought, and sold, like a horse or a pair of shoes.

But such thinking mystified American Indians. How could anyone possess a piece of earth? Land was like air, streams, the clouds—a blessing from the Great Spirit, or God, for all to use. When Indians spoke of their lands, they usually meant a place for the tribe, not individuals, a place that was borrowed temporarily, not possessed forever: "[T]hey valued it for the things it produced that sustained life," writes historian Janet A. McDonnell. "To Native Americans the land represented existence, identity, and a place of belonging."[20]

Conflict and Controversy

Understandably such differing concepts caused conflict and controversy between Indians and the English. Sometimes whites negotiated real estate deals with individual Indians who lacked authority to sell land for an entire tribe. Because most Indians could not read and did not understand legal contracts drawn up according to complicated principles of Anglo-Saxon jurisprudence, they often signed away all property rights when they intended to allow only occupancy, travel, or hunting privileges. Moreover land boundaries were often vague or poorly defined. In fact tribes often feuded among themselves over borders.

The English, inevitably, insisted that signed contracts or treaties were legally binding documents, giving them the right to take full permanent possession of the land in question.

Sometimes Indians and whites disputed each other's interpretations of "walking treaties," which set distances based on how far a man could walk in a day. Sometimes "riding treaties" were marked off by the amount of ground a rider on horseback could cover. Some Europeans infuriated the Indians by hiring specially trained people who could travel at astonishing rates.

In many cases, however, there was no misunderstanding at all. When the opportunities arose, the English and other whites simply took what they wanted. Usually American Indians were too weak and too disunited to stop them. Howard Zinn comments on this page of history:

> Behind the English invasion of North America, behind their massacre of Indians, their deception, their brutality, was that special powerful drive born in civilizations based on private property. It was a morally ambiguous drive; the need for space, for land, was a real human need. But in conditions of scarcity, in a barbarous epoch of history ruled by competition, this human need was transformed into the murder of whole peoples.[21]

2 Pushing the Indians West

Whether Indians fought back against intruding settlers or reacted peacefully, they invariably lost their lands to whites and had to move farther west.

These constant relocations caused Indians great mental and physical trauma,

Dutch traders barter manufactured goods for Indian handicrafts. Native Americans quickly became dependent on such trade, which made their lives much easier.

including hunger and illness. Still worse, they often came into conflict with tribes who already occupied the land. Forced removal kept many Native Americans perpetually unsettled and prevented them from staying in one place long enough to develop a way of life more compatible with European civilization.

How were the Europeans able to overwhelm the Indians? First of all, they eventually outnumbered Native Americans. Only about 180 whites lived at Plymouth and 1,200 in Jamestown in 1625. By 1670, however, the population of the English colonies was about 200,000. Seventy years later, this number had grown to 2 million.

In addition to greater numbers, the Europeans had better weapons, such as guns and pistols. These weapons were superior to spears, war clubs, and bows and arrows.

Europeans were more organized—using big armies to wage war. They developed disciplined militias and efficient local governments. Indians, on the other hand, had no standing armies. They fought mainly to seek revenge or to raid. Most Indian tribes were divided by ancient conflicts and rivalries.

Native Americans were indirectly weakened by commercial contacts with whites. White merchants traded the Indians beads, guns, hatchets, and a host of other useful

A settler offers alcohol to an Indian in trade. Native Americans' low tolerance for alcohol led to much abuse of the substance. Once inebriated, Indians were an easy mark for unscrupulous whites.

manufactured goods. Although Indians strengthened their fighting ability with advanced weapons, they began to lose the knowledge and survival skills of their ancestors and became more vulnerable to European control. Their dependency on whites also meant that they spent more time near white communities and became exposed to a slew of diseases brought by Europeans to the New World—measles, smallpox, plague, influenza, and others. Eventually, these diseases wiped out hundreds of thousands of Indians, who had lacked immunity to the bacteria and viruses that had come from abroad. These deaths clearly made it easier for whites to occupy new territories. When entire Indian villages in New England were destroyed by a plague in 1611 and 1612, the Puritan Cotton Mather observed: "The woods were almost cleaned of those pernicious creatures, to make room for a better growth."[22]

And in 1633, according to Governor Thomas Hutchinson, "the small pox made terrible havock among the Indians of Massachusetts. . . . They were destitute of every thing proper for comfort and relief and died in greater proportion than is known among the English."[23] In fact, Indians were so vulnerable to smallpox that between 100,000 and 300,000 eventually died from the disease. An estimated 130,000 Native Americans also died from the plague of 1781 and 1782. Clearly, diseases killed more native inhabitants of North America than bullets fired by whites.

The European newcomers also exposed Indians to something else that proved disastrous: alcoholic beverages. Native Americans were especially vulnerable to the ill effects of alcohol and became easy prey for unscrupulous white traders. Quaker leader William Penn observed:

Since Europeans came into these parts [Pennsylvania], they [the Indians] are grown great lovers of strong drink, rum especially, and for it exchange the richest of their skins and furs. If they are heated with liquor, they are restless till they have enough to sell; but when drunk, one of the most wretched spectacles in the world.[24]

Unscrupulous, land-hungry whites also learned to ply Indians with alcohol until they became irrationally drunk and agreed to make land concessions they never would have made while sober. Even Benjamin Franklin favored using rum "To extirpate [root out] these savages in order to make room for the cultivators of the earth [white farmers]."[25]

A Few Fair-Minded Whites

Not all encounters between America's native people and the English ended in violence. Roger Williams, the founder of

---

King Haglar Protests Strong Drink

Alcoholic beverages devastated the American Indian across the continent. As recorded in Native American Testimony, *edited by Peter Nabokov, in August 1754 King Haglar, a chieftain of the Carolina-based Catawbas, movingly pleaded with white traders to stop selling liquor to the youth of his tribe.*

"Brothers, here is one thing you yourselves are to blame very much in; that is you rot your grain in tubs, out of which you take and make strong spirits.

You sell it to our young men and give it [to] them, many times; they get very drunk with it [and] this is the very cause that they oftentimes commit those crimes that is offensive to you and us and all through the effect of that drink. It is also very bad for our people, for it rots their guts and causes our men to get very sick and many of our people has lately died by the effects of that strong drink, and I heartily wish you would do something to prevent your people from daring to sell or give them any of that strong drink, upon any consideration whatever, for that will be a great means of our being free from being accused of those crimes that is committed by our young men and will prevent many of the abuses that is done by them through the effects of that strong drink."

Quaker leader William Penn signs a treaty with Indians over land rights. Penn scrupulously upheld such agreements, earning the respect and affection of Native Americans.

Rhode Island, favored negotiating and compensating Indians for their properties. So did Quaker leader William Penn. In fact, Penn is said never to have broken a treaty with Indians during his acquisition of the land that would become Pennsylvania. The Indians so honored Penn's sincerity and integrity that they spoke of him with praise for generations.

"We meet on the broad pathway of good faith and good will," Penn told Delaware chief Tammany in 1682. "No advantage shall be taken on either side, but all shall be openness and love. We are the same as if one man's body was to be divided into two parts; we are of one flesh and blood."[26]

Tammany responded, "We will live in love with William Penn and his children as long as the creeks and rivers run, and while the sun, moon, and stars endure."[27]

According to historian Oliver Perry Chitwood, in *A History of Colonial America*:

These agreements were more important than those usually made between the red men and the whites because they were scrupulously observed by the Quaker settlers. They were also kept by the Indians, and for more than half a century the two races dwelt together in peace and maintained the most cordial relations. Penn traveled among the savages unarmed, and Quaker farmers would leave their children in care of Indians when they went away from home.[28]

When Williams and Penn died, however, the pattern of English aggression found outside Rhode Island and Pennsylvania became evident almost everywhere. When this happened, Indians allied themselves with the French against the English.

French and English Rivalry

By the late 1600s Holland and Spain were no longer major contenders for colonies in North America, leaving England and

France to fight each other for dominance. During this time period, continued immigration from Britain swelled the English colonies. By 1740 more than 1.5 million English settlers had arrived, making them the biggest European group in North America. This increase in population caused crowding in the colonies and spurred the demand for new lands.

Aggravating the situation was the presence of a natural border. The Appalachian Mountains, which run north and south for more than two thousand miles from Georgia to Maine, kept the growing colonial population penned between the mountain range and the Atlantic Ocean. Demand for new lands became so intense, however, that many settlers moved west beyond the Appalachians into uncharted Indian lands.

French explorers, trappers, and settlers had migrated south from Canada, also looking for new territory. For a long time, France and England had managed to avoid each other. Now, however, France's and England's territorial goals collided. The French wanted to keep the British out of the Ohio Valley, west of the Appalachians. The English desired this territory, plus all of French-held Canada.

Both the British and the French enlisted as allies various Indian tribes who mistakenly believed that their European partners would protect traditional hunting lands from settlement. But the Europeans were mainly interested in using Indians as pawns for their own power plays. A French missionary in Nova Scotia (then called Acadia), Abbé Jean-Louis Le Loutre, wrote to the French minister of Marine as follows:

As we cannot openly oppose the English venture, I think we cannot do better than to incite the Indians to continue warring on the English. My plan is to

---

Colonial Terror of Indian Attacks

Quoted in Daniel Boorstin's The Americans: The Colonial Experience *is Rev. Joseph Doddridge's firsthand reaction to Indian attacks in western Virginia in the late 1700s.*

"The Indian kills indiscriminately. His object is the total extermination of his enemies. Children are victims of his vengeance, because, if males, they may hereafter become warriors, or if females, they may become mothers. Even the fetal state is criminal in his view. It is not enough that the fetus should perish with the murdered mother, it is torn from her pregnant womb, and elevated on a stick or pole, as a trophy of victory and an object of horror to the survivors of the slain. If the Indian takes prisoners, mercy has but little concern in the transaction. He spared the lives of those who fall into his hands, for the purpose of . . . torture."

British soldiers unwittingly enter into an Indian ambush during the French and Indian War. Both England and France used Indian alliances during the war.

persuade the Indians to send word to the English that they will not permit new settlements to be made in Acadia. . . . I shall do my best to make it look to the English as if this plan comes from the Indians and that I have no part of it.[29]

Rivalry between England and France caused fighting to break out repeatedly throughout the 1600s and 1700s. The English named the last clash in 1754—a fight for control of the Ohio Valley—the French and Indian War.

As they watched whites inflict injury on each other, some Indian leaders suspected that once a single European power had come to dominate the New World, Native Americans could be the ultimate losers.

"Why do not you and the French fight in the old country and the sea?" Shingas the Delaware chief asked the British in 1758. "Why do you come to fight on our land? This makes everybody believe you want to take the land from us by force and settle it."[30]

During these early stages of the conflict, French forces repeatedly defeated

English troops. One of their notable successes was the defeat of the Virginia militia headed by Col. George Washington, as the colonists made their way to the French Fort Duquesne (now the site of Pittsburgh).

The tide of war changed in 1763, when high government officials in England at last dispatched enough military troops and supplies to enable the colonists to beat the French decisively and take control of Canada.

The defeat of France marked a turning point for the Indians: The British inherited much of North America.

In accordance with the Treaty of Paris of February 10, 1763, which marked the end of the war, France renounced all its land claims east of the Mississippi. At about the same time, in separate negotiations, Spain ceded Florida to England. Together, these land cessions meant that England commanded the entire eastern half of North America.

Indian Fear of the English

When the French fell from power in the New World, their former Indian allies—tribes along the Great Lakes and the Ohio River—feared that English settlers would swarm into the conquered areas, confiscate Indian lands, and punish the tribes who had warred against them.

Their fears were well founded, for English and colonial land investment companies soon moved west. The Ohio Company received 200,000 acres of land along the upper Ohio River from the British government. Another company, owned by a group of colonists that included George Washington, received 2.5 million acres in the Mississippi Valley to sell to settlers.

The white population flooded Indian lands, seizing them and prompting a religious uprising. An Indian prophet named Abnaki announced that the Great Spirit had sent him to warn Indians of a coming disaster. "I give you warning," he cried, "that if you suffer the Englishmen to dwell in your midst, their diseases and their poisons shall destroy you . . . and you shall die."[31]

Aroused by this prophecy, a powerful Ottawa leader named Pontiac attempted to consolidate the threatened tribes and stave off the white invasion. Messengers

Ottawa leader Pontiac launches a night attack on an English schooner that is protecting Fort Detroit. Pontiac hoped to lessen English settlement by aiding the French.

Pontiac counsels tribes on strategy against white Europeans. Pontiac was a remarkable leader, eventually uniting many tribes in the Algonquin family.

carried his call for unity to the Miamis, Ottawas, Chippewas, Wyandots, Potawatamis, Delawares, Shawnees, and others in the Algonquin family of Native Americans. They also delivered orders telling each of the tribes to attack nearby white settlements and forts at the end of May 1763.

"Why, says the Great Spirit, do you suffer these dogs in red clothing to enter your country and take the land I have given you?" Pontiac exclaimed. "Drive them from it! Drive them! When you are in distress I will help you!"[32]

Pontiac, however, had no illusions that his forces could compel the more powerful and numerous English to leave North America. Instead, he hoped to keep the English out of the Northwest by helping to restore the French to power.

In late May, Pontiac's forces hit Fort Detroit, causing terror throughout the frontier settlements of the English colonies. Slowly, the united tribal forces pushed the English settlers back toward the Alleghenies, killing nearly two thousand whites. "I mean to destroy the English and leave not one upon our lands," cried the Ottawa leader.[33]

This uprising—Pontiac's Rebellion— caused division among the American colonists. People in the East, who were not affected by the events on the Michigan peninsula, failed to give the matter the same degree of attention as the threatened pioneers on the frontier. Despite a rash of anti-Indian speechmaking, no colony provided aid to British troops.

But Pontiac failed in the end. No French aid ever materialized to help him. Nor could the many different tribes work together for an extended period of time. By 1766 the British had suppressed the rebellion. A military failure, Pontiac's war nevertheless caused shock waves of concern as far away as England.

The Proclamation of 1763

English authorities were so startled by the ferocity of the bloody attacks by Pontiac's forces that they decided to develop a strong land policy for Indians—the first of its kind. The new policy was embodied in a document called the Proclamation of 1763. Its main thrust was to prevent future clashes with Indians by keeping English settlers out of Indian territory.

The Proclamation of 1763 established a north–south line that followed the crest of the Appalachian Mountains, ranging from northern Georgia to Maine. Until official negotiations with Indians had taken place, English settlers were prohibited from settling west of the Appalachians— the Ohio Valley and the Great Lakes, otherwise known as the Northwest Territory, a region inhabited by the Ottawa, Chippewa, Shawnee, Potawatami, and other tribes.

The proclamation also stated that Indian tribes were independent nations and whites could not take their lands unless Indians had agreed to an exchange and were paid. Moreover, no longer could individual British colonies make treaties with Indians for land. Only agents acting on behalf of the government in London were authorized to participate in such dealings.

On paper the Proclamation of 1763 seemed like good news for American Indians living west of the Appalachians. At last, white officials recognized the plight of Native Americans. The English openly admitted, for example, that "Great frauds and abuses have been committed in the purchasing land of the Indians, to the great prejudice of our [English] interests, and to the great dissatisfaction of the . . . Indians."[34]

On the other hand, the proclamation sorely irritated and frustrated American colonists, who burned with desire for new lands. No imaginary line, they vowed, would prevent them from moving westward into Indian territory.

Many whites tried to use legal means to acquire Indian lands in the forbidden zone. Some, for example, obtained documents called "land warrants," which entitled the possessors to specified amounts of Indian land. Land warrants often were sold at low prices by British soldiers, who had received them as payment for military services rendered in Indian territory. Settlers who had purchased these warrants demanded that the mother country honor their claims by opening the forbidden Indian territories.

Thousands of other settlers ignored the proclamation and drove their wagons deep into Kentucky and western Pennsylvania.

Alarmed by the new influx of whites, members of the Delaware and Shawnee tribes met in 1768 with colonial representatives of New Jersey, Virginia, and Pennsylvania at Fort Stanwix, New York, to reach a peaceful solution. Here, Indians hoped to appease whites by agreeing to accept a new western boundary line for Indian lands—the Ohio River. A similar treaty negotiated with Cherokees in the same year in the settlement of Hard Labor and another in 1770 at Lochaber in present-day West Virginia, pushed the southern portions of the Proclamation line farther west.

Hordes of migrating whites paid no heed to the new treaties, however. Brazenly they crossed the Ohio River and the new southern borders, shot Indians, and staked land claims on Indian territories. In 1774 William Johnson, a British Indian agent, reported to the Lords of Trade in England:

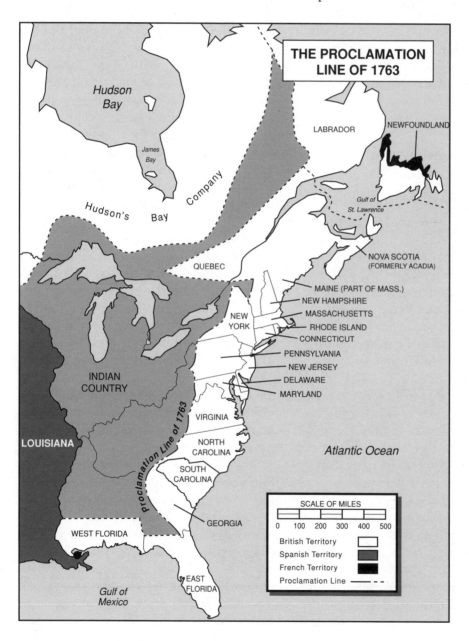

THE PROCLAMATION LINE OF 1763

Hudson Bay

James Bay

Hudson's Bay Company

LABRADOR

NEWFOUNDLAND

Gulf of St. Lawrence

QUEBEC

NOVA SCOTIA (FORMERLY ACADIA)

MAINE (PART OF MASS.)
NEW HAMPSHIRE
MASSACHUSETTS
RHODE ISLAND
CONNECTICUT
PENNSYLVANIA
NEW JERSEY
DELAWARE
MARYLAND

NEW YORK

INDIAN COUNTRY

Proclamation Line of 1763

VIRGINIA

NORTH CAROLINA

SOUTH CAROLINA

LOUISIANA

Atlantic Ocean

GEORGIA

WEST FLORIDA

EAST FLORIDA

Gulf of Mexico

SCALE OF MILES
0   100   200   300   400   500

British Territory
Spanish Territory
French Territory
Proclamation Line — — —

Once the English defeated the French, white settlers headed west in vast numbers, ignoring the Proclamation of 1763.

Everywhere on the frontier is found new encroachment by our people as cabins are being built on Indian lands beyond the established white limitations. Worse, they abuse and maltreat the Indians at every meeting. It seems as if the people are determined to bring a new war, though their own ruin may be the consequence.[35]

American settlers saw the situation differently. They were furious that the British had tried to stop their advances into Indian lands. The governor of Virginia, Lord Dunmore, expressed their point of view in 1774:

> The [Americans] . . . do not conceive that Government has any right to forbid their taking possession of a vast tract of country either uninhabited or which serves only as a shelter to a few scattered tribes of Indians.[36]

In fact, anger over the Proclamation of 1763 became so intense that it helped ignite a war with Britain in 1776—the American Revolution.

3 Pushed to the Mississippi

When America's War of Independence broke out in 1776, both the British and the Americans tried to enlist Indians as allies. Despite their distrust of the British in England, many Indians viewed the colonists on American soil as an even greater threat and threw their support to King George. But taking sides only further hurt the Indian cause. When the Iroquois tribes, for example, divided between the Americans and the British, they weakened their federation and became more vulnerable to revenge from either side. The Americans once burned forty Iroquois towns that had sided with the British. Among the burners was George Washington, whom the Indians nicknamed "the Town Destroyer."

In 1778 the Continental Congress negotiated a peace treaty with the Delawares—its first ever with an Indian tribe—that allowed

British soldiers attempt to convince Native Americans to side with them against the colonists. Such alliances always seemed to leave Indians at a disadvantage once whites settled the war.

American troops to pass through Delaware territory to reach British forts. Delawares also promised to help the Americans against the British. In return the Americans guaranteed the Delawares' own independent territory in the future. It was a promise never kept.

What may be the most important aspect of the treaty, however, is what it *did not* contain, for this omission influenced future American dealings with other tribes: namely, the Americans did not recognize any defined *boundaries* of Delaware territory.

In the peace treaty ending the war in 1783, however, the British recognized America's new boundaries: Canada to the north, the Mississippi River to the west, Florida (which was now back in Spanish hands and extended well west of present state boundaries, to the Mississippi River), and the Atlantic Ocean to the east.

What was the status of Indian lands in this vast territory? The United States claimed that Britain had ceded all land rights associated with the territory; therefore, all titles to Indian land and proclamations, such as the Proclamation of 1763, obtained during past dealings with the French and British were now void.

Writes noted scholar and Indian activist Vine Deloria Jr.:

> The United States laid claim to Great Britain's rights and responsibilities in protecting American Indians following the Revolution, and, although hardly a discoverer in the traditional sense, the United States adopted the doctrine of discovery as [the basis for how it dealt with Indians].[37]

The United States also took the position that although the ultimate title of the soil now rested with the federal government, Indians had a right to occupy and use Indian lands.

Meanwhile the individual states retained the capacity to deal with Indians within their respective borders, while the federal government assumed jurisdiction over all tribes living in the lands that were not states, lying west of the Appalachians to the Mississippi River.

Thus the stage was set for further American encroachment on Indian lands.

White Fear of Hostile Indians

White migration, however, was no easy matter. Many obstacles and perils awaited land-seizing settlers. Dangerous unmapped lands, hazardous or nonexistent roads and trails, wild animals, and bad weather all hindered travel along the frontier. According to historian Robert William Mondy, author of *Pioneers and Preachers: Stories of the Old Frontier*:

> Fear of hostile Indians also ranked high as a deterrent to frontier travel. In the vicinity of Pittsburgh, Pennsylvania, during the period between the French and Indian War and the close of the American Revolution, Indians were a constant threat to the traveler. Every farm house was a fortress. . . . There were few early settlers in the area who did not feel the effects of Indian revenge in some form. In one family, all members were killed and scalped. In another, a father and son were found dead, their bodies mutilated beyond recognition. In still another, the children were taken into captivity.[38]

The American frontier echoed with terrifying stories of Indian atrocities. Settlers knew that hostile Indians scalped, murdered, raped, and tortured their victims—both whites and other Native Americans—in exceedingly brutal ways. Mondy writes:

Indians knew how much pain the human body could endure without causing death. Corpses on their backs, arms and legs spread out and tied to bushes, trees, or stakes indicated the victims had died from starvation, thirst,

Indian Warfare Methods

James Smith was a rugged explorer, pioneer, woodsman, military officer, and white settler who had been reared by an Indian family on Pennsylvania's western frontier. From his adoptive family, he learned the ways of the Indian, including methods of warfare. This knowledge Smith later imparted to American fighters during the Revolutionary War. In 1799 he published a book about his life, which is excerpted in Voices from the Wilderness, *edited by Thomas Froncek.*

"I have often heard the British officers call the Indians the undisciplined savages, which is a capital mistake—as they have all the essentials of discipline. They are under good command, and punctual in obeying orders: they can act in concert, and when their officers lay a plan and give orders, they will cheerfully unite in putting all their directions into immediate execution; . . . When they go into battle they are not loaded or encumbered with many clothes, as they commonly fight naked, save only breech clout, leggins and mockesons. There is no such thing as corporeal punishment used, in order to bring them under such good discipline: degrading is the only chastisement [form of rebuke], and they are so unanimous in this, that it effectually answers the purpose. Their officers plan, order and conduct matters until they are brought into action, and then each man is to fight as though he was to gain the battle himself. General orders are commonly given in time of battle, either to advance or retreat, and is done by a shout or yell, which is well understood, and then they retreat or advance in concert. They are generally well equipped, and exceeding expert and active in the use of arms. . . .

They train up their boys to the art of war from the time they are twelve or fourteen years of age. . . . [B]ut were only part of our men taught this art, accompanied with our continental discipline, I think no European power . . . would venture to shew its head in the American woods."

Enraged by the many broken promises that whites had made to them, Indians began to attack white settlers encroaching on their land. Native Americans became frustrated and angry at the settlers' brazen attitudes.

rays of the sun, the sting of a thousand ants, or from other causes. Bodies of Indian victims displayed dislocations, artistic dissections, and split and broken toes and fingers. These victims had endured all imaginable horror, pain and fear.[39]

Stories of Indian abduction and torture slowed but did not halt westward migration into Indian lands.

The Northwest Ordinance

After the Revolutionary War, American citizens began to pressure their government to open Indian lands for white settlement, especially in the Northwest Territory—lands north of the Ohio River. (This area is now five states: Indiana, Michigan, Ohio, Illinois, and Wisconsin.)

To pave the way for new settlements, Congress passed the Land Ordinance of 1785, which carved up the territory into townships. The Northwest Ordinance of 1787 went even further by establishing the legal conditions necessary for settling the area and creating an official U.S. territory.

What was to happen to the Indians living there? On paper, the Northwest Ordinance made big promises:

The utmost good faith shall always be observed towards the Indians; their lands and property shall never be taken from them without their consent; and in their property, rights, and liberty, they shall never be invaded or disturbed, unless in just and lawful wars authorized by Congress.[40]

Such official assurance, however, meant almost nothing in practice. Despite the passage of the Northwest Ordinance and a series of other laws called trade and intercourse acts designed to protect the rights of Indians, the federal government did very little to prevent squatters, settlers, trappers, and adventurers from pouring into the Indian lands.

In 1790 settlers moved north of the Ohio River, believing they were on lands lawfully purchased by the United States the preceding year. A confederacy of tribes—the Shawnee, Miami, Potawatami, and Chippewa—saw things differently, however.

Led by a Miami named Little Turtle, the Indians furiously fought to drive the intruders out. President George Washington dispatched fourteen hundred federal troops into what is now Ohio to protect the settlers' claims. Along the Wabash River, however, the Americans suffered their worst defeat ever by Indians.

Four years of fighting passed until Washington found a military commander able to crush the Indians. Under the brilliant command of Maj. Gen. Wayne Anthony, the Americans defeated Little Turtle's forces at Fallen Timbers (near the present site of Toledo, Ohio) in mid-August.

Military leaders forced chiefs of the rebelling tribes to sign the Treaty of Greenville, which required them to cede most of present-day central and southern Ohio and parts of Indiana. The treaty also gave the Americans the right to purchase, when they pleased, the remainder of Indian lands east of the Mississippi and north of the Ohio River.

Britain Departs

In 1795 the United States successfully negotiated the removal to Canada of all British military forces present in the Northwest Territory. Now that Indian resistance was halted, and the Indians' major ally was gone from the region, American settlers felt free to relocate in the Ohio River valley. By 1800 roughly a million whites lived between the Mississippi River and the Appalachian Mountains, the landmark that had served as the Indian border only thirty-two years earlier.

But the settlers wanted more than just land; they wanted good land. And much of the good land in the Northwest Territory remained in Indian hands.

The Views of Thomas Jefferson

Although many U.S. leaders publicly professed that any lands acquired from Indians should be transferred in a legal manner, they seldom acted to protect Indians from land theft. In fact, they often changed their views to fit new political realities as white settlement became a popular idea. For example, Thomas Jefferson, who became president in 1801, wrote to a European correspondent in 1806: "It may be regarded as certain that not a foot of land will ever be taken from the Indians without their own consent. The sacredness of their rights is felt by all thinking persons in America as much as in Europe."[41]

But at the same time, Jefferson could express the opposite view. In another letter he observed:

When [the Indians] withdraw themselves to the culture of a small piece of land, they will perceive how useless to them are their extensive forests, and will be willing to pare them off from time to time in exchange for necessaries for their farms and families. To promote this disposition to exchange lands which they have to spare and we want, we shall push our trading houses, and be glad to see the good and influential [Indian] individuals among them run into debt, because we observe that when these debts get beyond what the individuals can pay, they become willing to lop them off by a cession of lands.[42]

Thomas Jefferson initially advocated peaceful and equitable acquisition of Indian lands. In his zeal to populate the United States "from sea to shining sea" however, Jefferson advocated more violent methods.

Six years later, Jefferson's views hardened even more against the very Indians he once had vowed to protect. He wrote: "We shall be obliged to drive them with the beasts of the forests into the stony mountains."[43]

Jefferson Expands the United States

In 1803 Thomas Jefferson negotiated the biggest real estate deal in history. For $15 million, he bought from France the so-called Louisiana Territory, a huge expanse of North American land that dwarfs the present state of Louisiana.

What Jefferson purchased represented one-third of North America. For four cents an acre, he added to the United States lands that became the states of Louisiana, Arkansas, Oklahoma, Missouri, North and South Dakota, Iowa, Nebraska, Kansas, Minnesota, Colorado, Wyoming, and Montana. At one stroke, the United States doubled in size.

The Louisiana Purchase also gave the United States ownership of the Mississippi River, which gave settlers even more access to the lands between the great river and the Appalachian Mountains.

Initially, Jefferson thought his purchase offered a solution to the gnawing problem of the presence of Indians in the Northwest Territory. The president hoped to persuade these Indians to leave their ancestral lands and settle in the Louisiana Territory. That they might collide with other Native Americans already living in Louisiana did not seem to have occurred to him.

American officials put Jefferson's ideas into action by subjecting the tribal chiefs

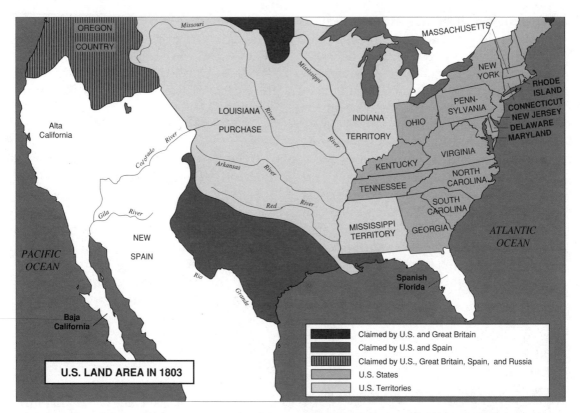

Claimed by U.S. and Great Britain
Claimed by U.S. and Spain
Claimed by U.S., Great Britain, Spain, and Russia
U.S. States
U.S. Territories

U.S. LAND AREA IN 1803

not to military force but to strong negotiating pressure. Browbeaten, outnumbered, and overwhelmed by aggressive white settlers, tribes one by one concluded that they had little choice, short of war, but to comply with U.S. treaty makers. This meant giving up their land for money, food and supplies, and the promise of new homes west of the Mississippi.

Tecumseh

One of the principal treaty negotiators for the Americans was William Henry Harrison, superintendent of the Northwest Indians and governor of Indian Territory. Harrison had only disdain for Indians. Like many other whites, he viewed them

as lowly beings who impeded American progress. In a speech before the Indiana legislature in 1810, he cried out:

> Is one of the fairest portions of the globe to remain in a state of nature, the haunt of a few wretched savages, when it seems destined, by the Creator, to give support to a large population, and to be the seat of civilization, of science, and true religion?[44]

Harrison wrested control of much of Indian Territory from Indians by negotiating fifteen separate treaties that required Indians to hand over a huge part of present-day Ohio, the rest of Indiana and Illinois, and sections of Wisconsin and Michigan—all for about a penny per acre. Critics contend that Harrison used stealth and deceit in some of these dealings.

Shawnee chief Tecumseh corners Gen. William Harrison. Tecumseh resisted Harrison's efforts to gain more land through treaties with the Indians.

One of Harrison's attempts to obtain a treaty incurred an angry response from a powerful Shawnee chief named Tecumseh. "Sell a country!" thundered Tecumseh. "Why not sell the air, the cloud and the great sea?"[45]

Strong, imaginative, forceful, Tecumseh was a veteran of Little Turtle's uprising. He was also a compelling speaker, a leader respected by Indians and whites alike. Even Tecumseh's avowed enemy, Harrison himself, praised the Shawnee chief's greatness: "He is one of those uncommon geniuses which spring up occasionally to produce revolutions and overturn the established order of things."[46]

Although neither Jefferson nor the next three American presidents relied on military force to remove Indians, Tecumseh and other chiefs believed that eventually the United States would try to oust them and forcibly send them west.

Tecumseh had a serious personal reason to be cynical. His father and an older brother had been killed trying to prevent whites from taking Indian land. Afterward, Tecumseh vowed to train himself to become a war leader and to create a vast confederacy of Indians—one larger than any ever tried before—to stop the relentless white assault on Indian lands.

Journeying from Florida to the Canadian Great Lakes, Tecumseh convinced a galaxy of tribes to unite against the corrupting influence of white culture and power:

The way, the only way to stop this evil [the white man's ways] is for the red men to unite in claiming a common and equal right in the land, as it was at first, and should be now—for it was never divided, but belonged to all.[47]

Tecumseh became the confederacy's political leader, and his twin brother—a mystic named Tenskwatawa, who was known as the Prophet—served as spiritual head.

Warily watching Tecumseh build his confederacy, Harrison decided that he would have to attempt to destroy the Indian alliance soon, before it became too powerful. In November 1811, Harrison got his chance when Tecumseh left the area with his best warriors, trying to round up support for his proposed alliance. While the Indians' power to resist was at its lowest, Harrison mustered a thousand men and marched on Prophet's Town—an Indian stronghold on the Wabash River, near Tippecanoe Creek, in Indiana.

The result was a devastating defeat for the Indians. Harrison's forces burned Prophet's Town and scattered the surviving warriors. Tecumseh's dream of a unified Indian resistance was shattered.

Tecumseh, though, had one last hope: that an unlikely ally, the British, could defeat the United States in yet another white man's war.

"The Americans we must fight, not the English," Tecumseh now told his Indian allies. "The Americans are our eternal foes, the hungry devourers of the country of our fathers."[48]

A Turning Point: The War of 1812

When the U.S. Congress convened in 1811, many representatives clamored for war against Britain. These "war hawks," coming mainly from the western and southern re-

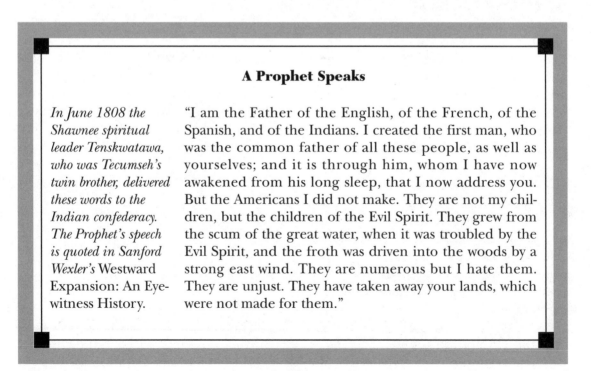

A Prophet Speaks

In June 1808 the Shawnee spiritual leader Tenskwatawa, who was Tecumseh's twin brother, delivered these words to the Indian confederacy. The Prophet's speech is quoted in Sanford Wexler's Westward Expansion: An Eyewitness History.

"I am the Father of the English, of the French, of the Spanish, and of the Indians. I created the first man, who was the common father of all these people, as well as yourselves; and it is through him, whom I have now awakened from his long sleep, that I now address you. But the Americans I did not make. They are not my children, but the children of the Evil Spirit. They grew from the scum of the great water, when it was troubled by the Evil Spirit, and the froth was driven into the woods by a strong east wind. They are numerous but I hate them. They are unjust. They have taken away your lands, which were not made for them."

Tecumseh was a remarkable leader. Realizing that the only way to oppose European settlement was to forge a union of Native American tribes, Tecumseh became a shrewd diplomat, eventually convincing many tribes to join his alliance.

napped thousands of them, forcing them into service in the Royal Navy.

Many Americans were also convinced that the British were arming Indians in Canada to raid settlers in the United States.

The war hawks cited all these grievances to support their successful call for war against Britain in 1812. In that year Tennessee congressman Felix Grundy boasted:

> We shall drive the British from our continent—they will no longer have an opportunity of intriguing with our Indian neighbors, and setting on the ruthless savages to tomahawk our women and children. That nation will lose her Canadian trade, and, by having no resting place in this country, her means of annoying us will be diminished.[49]

But the war hawks also wanted something else—the expansion of American territory. They saw war as a means of grabbing Canada and Florida and adding these territories to the growing American empire.

From the onset of the War of 1812, as it was called, the British goal was to keep the United States from expanding westward—a plan that dovetailed with Tecumseh's desire to hold back the incoming tide of American pioneers.

Thus, side by side, the British and Tecumseh's Indian alliance fought the Americans in the regions of Lake Erie and Lake Michigan.

Indian Land Loss After the War of 1812

A treaty ending the War of 1812 was signed in 1814, but the fighting had settled nothing substantial between the Americans and the

gions of the United States, believed that the country had to fight to right several wrongs inflicted by the British.

The causes for anti-British feelings were complex. A smoldering dislike for Britain, predating the Revolution, still lingered among many Americans. Anger also flared when Americans learned that the British had intercepted and seized neutral American merchant ships headed for France, which was at war with Britain. Worse yet, the British claimed that American sailors were British deserters and kid-

British. "The real losers were the Indians," argues historian Rebecca Brooks Gruver. "After suffering heavy casualties, they no longer had any promise of British firearms or supplies. In effect, they were left to the mercy of the land-hungry American people."[50]

Everywhere, the situation for Indians looked bleak. In 1813 Tecumseh died in battle, his Indian confederacy smashed. Making matters worse, the Tennessee militia led by Gen. Andrew Jackson vanquished Creek forces at the Battle of Horseshoe Bend in Alabama in 1814. The Creeks were forced to cede twenty-three million acres to the United States.

This collapse of Indian resistance meant easier passage for white settlers moving west. Also, improved steamboats, canals, and roadways enabled more settlers to move to the west faster and more easily than ever before. Many of the latest migrants were former maritime workers who had lost their jobs in the Northeast when the war disrupted commercial shipping.

The War of 1812 was also a turning point for the Americans concerning their attitude over their own national identity. Large numbers of the settlers were European-born immigrants who thus far had lacked a strong sense of loyalty to any state or, for that matter, to the new national government. But the War of 1812 awakened a powerful sense of belonging in many settlers, who now felt more "American" in their outlook.

"The war has renewed and reinstated the national feelings and character which the Revolution had given," observed U.S.

Tecumseh dies in battle at the hands of Americans. The dream of an Indian alliance died with him.

Americans' victory over the British in the War of 1812 led to a renewed sense of national identity and an increased lack of tolerance for Indian occupation of North American territory.

Treasury secretary Albert Gallatin. "The people now have more general objects of attachment. . . . They are more American; they feel and act more as a nation."[51]

This new surge of national loyalty also prompted people to look to the federal government for an improved transportation system, cheap land to settle, and above all protection from hostile Indians. Settlers and would-be settlers exerted tremendous political pressure on their government to cancel Indian titles to land in the Northwest Territory.

In response, the government sent commissioners to negotiate with one tribe after another to obtain the lands. Now that Indian power was weakened, if not gone in the Northwest Territory, the demoralized tribes had little choice but to comply with U.S. demands and move farther west.

But in the South, several powerful Indian nations—the Cherokees, Chickasaws, Choctaws, Creeks, and Seminoles—remained on their native lands. For the time being, the federal government lacked the power to oust them.

This situation would change soon.

4 Forced Removal Begins

In late 1825 President James Monroe proposed that all Indians be removed from their homes and relocated west of the Mississippi River. "Experience has clearly demonstrated," the president said, "that, in their present state, it is impossible to incorporate [the Indians] in such masses, in any form whatever, into our system. . . . The great object to be accomplished is, the removal of those tribes."[52]

Such a removal, argued Monroe, offered many obvious "advantages" not only to the United States, but to the Indians as well. Benefits to whites were obvious. But what advantage could Indians expect? For one thing, assured the president, they could avoid "wars between them and the United States."[53]

Monroe had in mind a huge undertaking: the relocation of an estimated ninety-seven thousand Native Americans who lived in North Carolina, Georgia, Alabama, Tennessee, Ohio, Indiana, Illinois, Missouri, New York, and the Arkansas and Michigan territories.

The physical work in relocating so many people was daunting. But there were other problems, too. Indian resistance to removal might prove bloody and expensive. Plus, there were legal and ethical problems to consider. For example, many tribes in the areas targeted for removal resided on land the United States had promised was theirs "forever."

The idea of Indian removal became increasingly popular across the nation, but especially in the South. Whites there lusted for the rich Cherokee, Chickasaw, Creek, Choctaw, and Seminole homelands. Together, these Indian nations were nicknamed the Five Civilized Tribes, because

President James Monroe contributed to the relocation of Native Americans by suggesting that they be moved west of the Mississippi River. He believed this would end conflicts between Native Americans and whites.

Part of the Five Civilized Tribes, the Creek were prime targets for whites eager to take over their lucrative farmland.

they exhibited certain cultural patterns considered to represent civilization: sedentary living, permanent homes, farming, and organized government. The Cherokees ran schools and printed a newspaper in their own alphabet.

Despite their best efforts to live in the European-American tradition, however, the Five Civilized Tribes could not prevent whites from attempting to confiscate their tribal lands.

The Era of Andrew Jackson

Many southern whites were encouraged in 1828 by the election to the presidency of Andrew Jackson, a fabled Indian fighter, as problems with Native Americans in Georgia, Mississippi, and Alabama had reached a boiling point. Each of these states had outlawed tribal governments, confiscating large tracts of Indian land and opening them to white settlement. In Georgia, for instance, the government gave away vast

stretches of land to white settlers as lottery prizes.

Mobs of white settlers and speculators, either encouraged or ignored by state officials, squatted on lands that remained in tribal hands. They attacked Indians, sold

Convinced that the Cherokee could only compete with whites if they became literate, Sequoyah invented an alphabet that was used by all members of the tribe.

President Andrew Jackson was a staunch advocate of Indian relocation and proposed the Indian Removal Act. A former Indian fighter, he believed whites were entitled to Indian lands.

them liquor, and bullied, bribed, or cheated them out of land.

The clamor for Cherokee lands rose to a fever pitch in 1829, when gold was discovered in northern Georgia. As squatters and prospectors poured into the area, Cherokees appealed to the U.S. government for protection. No assistance ever came, even though the Cherokees had federal law on their side. According to the Indian Trade and Intercourse Act of 1802, for example, Indians could be dispossessed of their lands only by treaty. This law further stated that only the *federal* government had the authority to regulate Indian affairs.

Advocates of Indian removal, however, received federal help in 1830 when Jackson proposed the Indian Removal Act, which called for the relocation of all Indians to the west side of the Mississippi River, where they would be given new lands in exchange for those in the South that had been guaranteed to them forever, then taken from them.

Such a move, insisted Jackson, was the best way to protect southern Indians from the assaults of land-hungry squatters and speculators. The bill stated that if necessary, the United States would protect native people and enforce the rules by removing intruders. Jackson's plan also assured Indians that their new homes would never be incorporated into any state or territory.

Jackson's bill drew applause from many supporters in Congress; but other legislators were appalled. Senator Theodore Frelinghuysen of New Jersey angrily declared, "We have crowded the tribes upon a few miserable acres of our Southern frontier; it is all that is left to them of their once boundless forests; and still, like the horse leech, our insatiated cupidity cries, give! give! give!"[54]

Many Americans, particularly members of religious groups such as the Society of Friends (Quakers), strongly opposed the bill and pressured their legislators to vote against it. But after weeks of tumultuous debate, Congress passed the relocation bill by the narrow margin of 103 to 97. Noted Jackson historian Robert V. Remini reports the aftermath:

The reaction of the American people to removal was predictable. Some were outraged. Others seemed uncomfortable with it but agreed that it had to be done. Probably a large number of Americans favored removal and applauded the President's action in settling the Indian problem once and for all. In short, there was no overwhelming public outcry against it.[55]

Peter Nabokov, editor of *Native American Testimony*, continues the story:

Now, the President . . . had both the power to select the tribes that were to be removed and the money—half a million dollars [provided by Congress]—to finance the giant exodus. To present an illusion of tribal consent, Jackson's secret agents bribed, deceived, and intimidated individual Indians, falsified records, squelched open debate, and finally persuaded some tribesmen to sign in favor of removal.[56]

Jackson signed the Indian Removal Act into law on May 28, 1830, drawing an eloquent written protest from the Cherokees.

The Choctaws and the Chickasaws

The first tribe to feel the heavy hand of the United States was the Choctaw, in Mississippi. Although most of the twenty thousand Choctaws opposed removal plans, the tribal representatives who met with U.S. officials succumbed to bribery and signed the Treaty of Dancing Rabbit Creek, which required the Choctaws to abandon their homes and give up 10.5 million acres to the U.S. government.

In late 1831 the first phase of a four-hundred-mile journey began for the Choctaw. Traveling in ox wagons, on horseback, and on foot, part of the tribe—thirteen thousand anguished men, women, and children—were escorted by armed white soldiers to make sure they did not falter along the way.

An Indian village is routed by white soldiers. The Indian Removal Act, signed into law in 1830, gave the United States complete power to remove Indians off their land. Any Indian tribe that opposed removal was treated harshly.

Eyewitness to Heartbreak

Alexis de Tocqueville, the great French observer of nineteenth-century American life, recorded his personal witness of heartbreak and misery of the Choctaw removal in his classic book, Democracy in America.

"At the end of the year 1831 I was on the left bank of the Mississippi, at the place the Europeans called Memphis. While I was there a numerous band of Choctaws . . . arrived; these savages were leaving their country and seeking to pass over to the right bank of the Mississippi, where they hoped to find an asylum promised to them by the American government. It was then the depths of winter, and that year the cold was exceptionally severe; the snow was hard on the ground, and huge masses of ice drifted on the river. The Indians brought their families with them; there were among them the wounded, the sick, newborn babies, and the old men on the point of death. They had neither tents nor wagons, but only some provisions and weapons. I saw them embark to cross the great river, and the sight will never fade from my memory. Neither sob nor complaint rose from that silent assembly. Their afflictions were of long standing, and they felt them to be irremediable. All the Indians had already got into the boat that was to carry them across; their dogs were still on the bank; as soon as the animals finally realized that they were being left behind forever, they all together raised a terrible howl and plunged into the icy waters of the Mississippi to swim after their masters."

The relocation became a prolonged death march. Winter was unusually severe that year, with temperatures often dropping below zero. Pneumonia killed Choctaws of all ages. When warm weather appeared, a deadly cholera epidemic claimed hundreds of victims. Making matters even worse, the government contractors and federal agents responsible for the well-being of the Indians during the removal cheated them in transactions for food and supplies.

Two thousand Indians died as a result of the removal. Knowing of this ordeal, the remaining Choctaws in Mississippi refused to follow their fellow tribesmen. Instead, they clung to their homelands, despite an ever-increasing tide of invading white settlers who arrived and staked claims on Choctaw land.

In 1850 several Choctaws who had remained in Mississippi described their plight in a letter to a white friend:

Our tribe has been woefully imposed upon of late. We have had our habitations torn down and burned; our fences destroyed, cattle turned into our fields & we ourselves have been scourged [whipped], manacled [handcuffed], fettered [tied up] and otherwise personally abused until by such treatment some of our best men have died. These are the acts of those persons who profess to be the agents of the Government to procure our removal to the Arkansas and who cheat us out of all they can by the use of fraud, duplicity, and even violence.[57]

The army had much less trouble with the Chickasaws. Overrun by white settlers in Mississippi, many of these Native Americans had already migrated west several years before. Those left behind signed away their lands and also headed west.

The Cherokees Go to Court

Georgia's Cherokees, however, resisted. Instead of waging war, they turned to a defense often used by the white man: the legal system.

In fact, a legal dispute over Georgia land had brewed for many years. In 1802 the federal government had promised to abolish Indian land titles in the state of Georgia. The Cherokees, however, pointed to their own treaty with the United States, signed in 1785, which guaranteed Cherokee lands and made them off-limits to non-Indians. Two similar treaties followed—one in 1791 and another in 1797—reaffirming the boundary lines of Cherokee land.

In 1827 the Cherokees antagonized whites by proclaiming themselves an independent nation in northwest Georgia. The state lawmakers, however, declared the Cherokee nation to be null and void in 1832 and extended Georgia laws over the Cherokees. New Georgia laws required Indians to serve in the military and to pay taxes, even though they were denied civil rights: They could not testify in court or hold public meetings. They were not even allowed to mine gold on their own lands.

Realizing the futility of taking up arms against a white society that greatly outnumbered and could easily overpower them, the Cherokees hired William Wirt, a former U.S. attorney general, to represent their interests before the U.S. Supreme Court.

In an attempt to prevent Georgia from enforcing state laws against his clients, Wirt argued that the Cherokee tribe had the status of a foreign nation and as such should be protected from the Georgia government's attempt to impose its laws.

Not so, responded Chief Justice John Marshall in October 1832, in *Cherokee Nation v. Georgia*. The Indians, he wrote, were "domestic dependent nations," or wards of the United States, not independent foreign nations. Despite this distinction and plenty of pro-Indian language by Marshall in the decision, the Court refused to issue the requested injunction, an order that would have stopped the state of Georgia from applying its laws to the Cherokee.

Another case involving the Cherokee came before the Supreme Court in 1832. Ten white missionaries who were sympathetic to the Cherokees had deliberately violated a Georgia law requiring any white person to obtain a permit before entering Indian territory and to swear allegiance to the state of Georgia.

A Georgia militia arrested the missionaries, beat them, and marched them to a county jail. There was a trial, a jury convicted the prisoners, and the court meted out four-year prison sentences. Dr. Elizur Butler and Samuel Worcester appealed their convictions to the U.S. Supreme Court. This time, in *Worcester v. Georgia*, Marshall ruled that the Georgia law used against the plaintiffs was unconstitutional and that the missionaries should be set free.

President Jackson called the Supreme Court's decision "too preposterous" and ignored it. "John Marshall has made his opinion," the former Indian fighter allegedly said. "Now let him enforce it."[58]

The Trail of Tears

The Cherokees' ongoing legal efforts won them nothing except a delay in relocation. But time ran out in 1836. In New Echota, Georgia, tribal strife broke out when the Cherokees learned that a small group of their own men, having met with white officials, had signed a treaty calling for removal of all Cherokees. Many Cherokees angrily protested this action and repudiated the treaty, vowing never to leave Georgia.

By 1838, however, Jackson's successor, Martin Van Buren, had ordered the U.S. Army to remove the Cherokees from their

A Plea for Help

Anguished by their treatment at the hands of Georgia legislators, Andrew Jackson, and the federal government, the Cherokees made a public appeal for justice with the Memorial and Protest of June 22, 1836. This excerpt is from a passage quoted in The National Experience: A History of the United States, *by John Blum and five other distinguished American historians.*

"The Cherokees were happy and prosperous . . . [under earlier, properly observed treaties with the government of the United States] and . . . they made rapid advances in civilization, morals, and in the arts and sciences. Little did they anticipate, that when taught to think and feel as the American citizen, and to have with him a common interest, they were to be despoiled by their guardian, to become strangers and wanderers in the land of their fathers, forced to return to the savage life, and to seek a new home in the wilds of the far west, and that without their consent. An instrument purporting to be a treaty with the Cherokee people, has recently been made public by the President of the United States, that will have such an operation, if carried into effect. This instrument, . . . [we] aver before the civilized world, and in the presence of Almighty God, is fraudulent, false upon its face, made by unauthorized individuals, without the sanction, and against the wishes, of the great body of the Cherokee people."

and wasted by disease, exposure, and starvation, nearly four thousand Cherokees—almost one-fourth of all tribal members—died during the exodus.

Creeks Driven Out

In 1832 the Creeks watched their remaining landholdings become overrun by white squatters. That same year, tribal leaders signed the Washington Treaty, which required them to give up five million acres of tribal land. Another two million acres were redistributed to Creeks on an individual, rather than a tribal, basis. Indians who refused the allotted land migrated to the newly designated Indian Territory west of the Mississippi.

Within days whites illegally appeared on the newly distributed Creek lands to establish homesteads. The federal government did nothing to stop them. Instead, it imposed another treaty on the Creeks, forcing them to accept total removal.

After a band of outraged Creeks attacked encroaching white settlers, the U.S. Army swept into the area and hunted down all Creeks—hostile and peaceful alike—and rounded them up for deportation. Those suspected of involvement in the armed attack were manacled and chained.

In 1836, under military guards, fifteen thousand Creek men, women, and children were marched at gunpoint off their lands for a long journey of death and disease out west. Half the Creek nation either died along the way or perished from sickness, hunger, and heartbreak during the first years after their arrival in newly established Indian Territory.

Chief Justice John Marshall ruled in 1832 that the Cherokee were not a separate nation and could be removed from their lands by the U.S. government.

Georgia homelands, by force if necessary. In May armed state and federal troops flooded into northern Georgia, surrounded seventeen thousand Cherokees, ordered them to evacuate their homes immediately, and forced them into concentration camps. Within a week, the shocked Cherokee were forced at gunpoint to prepare for the upcoming treacherous thousand-mile journey from Georgia to Indian Territory. The route they would take is now called the Trail of Tears.

On October 1, 1838, the first wave of 645 wagons, filled with weeping Cherokees and their hastily grabbed possessions rolled westward. White Georgians eagerly rushed in to claim the abandoned lands, sometimes before an area had been totally vacated.

Broken in spirit and body, exhausted,

Once the Cherokee lost their legal battle to retain their lands, they were loaded into wagons at gunpoint and forced to make the trek west of the Mississippi. Their relocation resulted in the death of one-fourth of their tribal members.

Defining the New Indian Lands

Although the government began deporting southern Indians in 1831, it did not legally define the dimensions of the new Indian Territory until three years later: The lands included all of the United States west of the Mississippi "and not within the States of Missouri and Louisiana or the Territory of Arkansas."[59] These Indian lands were forbidden to most whites. But, writes Indian historian Dee Brown,

a new wave of white settlers swept westward and formed the territories of Wisconsin and Iowa. This made it necessary for the policy makers in Washington to shift the "permanent Indian frontier" from the Mississippi River to the 95th Meridian [which runs north and south and is roughly marked by present-day Kansas City].[60]

And to keep the newly relocated Indians confined west of the new dividing line and to stop white settlers from encroaching into the Indian Territory, the U.S. government established a string of military posts to police the border.

Armed Resistance in Illinois

Southern Indians were not the only ones to be removed in the 1830s. To the north, in 1832, Chief Black Hawk led bands of Sac and Fox east across the Mississippi to Illinois—a region from which they had been removed earlier by the United States. Desperately hungry, the Indians crossed back into familiar lands searching for food. But their presence in Illinois terrified white settlers and prompted the governor to call on President Andrew Jackson for military assistance.

Help arrived in the combined form of state militia and U.S. Army troops, which fought the Indians in a series of skirmishes

Ousting the Cherokee

This excerpt from a letter written by Capt. L. B. Webster to his wife on June 9, 1838, as quoted in Thomas E. Mails's The Cherokee People, *reveals the distress felt by one army officer in carrying out his government's decision to forcibly remove Cherokees from their homelands.*

"We are said to be in the thickest settled portion of the Cherokee country, and the least civilized. There are about six thousands in our neighborhood—their houses are quite thick about us, and they all remain quietly at home at work on their little farms, as though no evil was intended them. They sell us very cheap anything they have to spare, and look upon the regular troops as their friends. . . . These are the innocent and simple people, into whose houses we are to obtrude ourselves, and take off by force. They have no idea of fighting, but submit quietly to be tied and led away. If there is anything that goes against my conscience it is this work, and I would not do it, whatever might be the consequences, did I not know that there are thousands that would, and probably with much less feeling towards the poor creatures. . . . Orders are out to begin operations on the 12th. . . . I expect to see many affecting scenes before the business is over. Those that were in Georgia have already been collected, and sent to the principal depots, from whence they are sending to the West as fast as possible."

To force Black Hawk and members of the Sac and Fox tribe back across the Mississippi, U.S. militia and army troops were brought in to fight them. The Battle of Bad Axe is pictured.

and finally drove them back to the other side of the Mississippi.

After the so-called Black Hawk War, Andrew Jackson gave in to the demands of settlers outraged by the arrival of the Indians and ordered the relocation to the Indian Territory of all other tribes still living in the Northwest. All but nine thousand Native Americans eventually were driven out.

Seminole Wars

Florida Seminoles vowed to fight Jackson's troops rather than submit to forced removal in 1835. This was not the first time they had defied Andrew Jackson. The Seminoles had met him in battle in 1818, when he was a general leading a foray into Spanish-held West Florida. That mission had consisted of attacking strongholds of escaped runaway black slaves, and Seminoles who had been raiding white settlements on the American side of the border.

Chief Black Hawk defied U.S. orders and led Sac and Fox back east across the Mississippi when the Indians became desperately hungry.

Though relative newcomers to Florida, many Seminoles nonetheless held Spanish land grants to territory in the area. Moreover, according to the treaty by which Spain had initially ceded Florida to the United States in 1819, all inhabitants of the territory were entitled to all the rights of other U.S. citizens.

Whites had scorned such legalities when the United States took control of Florida, however, and to hasten the opening of Florida lands to white settlers, the new government had "negotiated" with seventy Seminole chiefs and signed the 1823 Treaty of Camp Moultrie. This agreement called for the Seminoles to vacate coastal lands, as well as most of West Florida, and to resettle south of the headwaters of the St. Johns River and east of Tampa Bay—that is, in the central part of the state. Under these terms, the Seminoles had lost thirty million acres of land.

In 1827 the Florida Legislative Council had declared that any male found outside the territory delimited in the Treaty of Camp Moultrie "shall receive not exceeding thirty-nine stripes on his bare back and his gun be taken away from him."[61]

American settlers were soon dissatisfied with even this arrangement, however, demanding more Florida land and urging that the Seminoles be pushed out of the way. "The present location [of the Indians] is in the pathway of our settlers," complained the council in 1829, "and has seriously impeded the settlement of the fairest part of Florida."[62]

Not long after Jackson had signed the Indian Removal Act in 1830, the federal government began pressuring the Seminoles to vacate the lands granted them by the Treaty of Camp Moultrie.

Osceola led Seminoles in a fight to preserve their lands. For eight years, the Seminoles attacked and murdered white settlers who had moved onto Seminole land.

Beginning in 1835, however, a fierce leader named Osceola led the Seminoles in a rebellion. For the next eight years, the Seminoles attacked, raided, and murdered settlers throughout north-central Florida.

By 1842, though, Seminole power had begun to weaken. Osceola was imprisoned and three thousand Seminoles were captured and transported west. The fighting faded away in 1843, as a few defiant bands of Seminoles evaded federal troops and hid in the vast South Florida Everglades, abandoning their most desirable lands to whites.

White troops attack Seminoles in retaliation for Seminole attacks on whites. Although whites were able to wrest away most of the desirable Seminole land, a few defiant bands resisted white settlement by hiding in Florida swampland.

Jackson's Legacy

Although Andrew Jackson was no longer president when the Cherokee death marches and the bloody Seminole resistance occurred, he did see the effects of the many profound changes due to his policy of relocation. By 1836 Jackson had ordered the relocation west of the Mississippi of a total of 45,690 Indians. He also added 100 million acres of Indian land to the United States.

Jackson's policy led to the death of an estimated thirty thousand Indian men, women, and children—either en route to resettlement areas or during the first few years in the western territories.

Jackson had argued that once relocated beyond the Mississippi, Indians could live unmolested and in peace forever, far from whites. Nothing could have been further from the truth. White settlers had no intention of staying out of Indian territory for very long. The French writer Alexis de Tocqueville made this observation in the 1830s:

> I think the Indian race is doomed to perish, and I cannot prevent myself from thinking that on the day when the Europeans shall be established on the coasts of the Pacific Ocean, it will cease to exist.[63]

Chapter

5 The Disappearing Frontier

Life proved hard for the relocated tribes in the Indian Territory. The new lands seemed strange and forbidding. Blistering hot in summer, freezing in winter, they could also be inundated with floods, as the Choctaws learned in June 1833, when they experienced one of the worst floods of the Arkansas River in history. Families were wiped out, possessions lost, corn crops destroyed. Flies multiplied in the filthy waters. Diseases swept through the tribe.

"Not a family but more or less sick; the Choctaws dying to an alarming extent. . . ," observed Francis W. Armstrong, a Choctaw agent and acting superintendent of Indian Affairs for the Western Territory. "Near the agency there are 3,000 Indians and within the hearing of a gun from this spot 100 have died within five weeks."[64]

Tribal Conflicts

Making life even grimmer were the tribal conflicts that invariably arose among Native Americans already dwelling in Indian Territory and newly arrived tribes. The Chickasaws, for example, were unable to settle permanently for at least four years because the federal government failed to make the area safe from raids by "wild" Indians, such as the Delawares, Shawnees, Kickapoos, Caddoes, and Keechies.

During this time, wrote Grant Foreman, a leading authority on removal,

the Chickasaws led a restless, unsettled life on the lands of the Choctaw Indians with no incentive nor opportunity to establish their government, schools, and other institutions, nor land upon which they could build their homes. To aggravate the demoralization resulting from their forced migration, the emigrants on the way through Arkansas contracted smallpox from which between 500 and 600 of their tribe died before the disease was checked by vaccination.[65]

At times, trouble arose among the Five Civilized Tribes. For instance, because the Seminoles resisted removal, the federal government punished them by forcing them to live with the Creeks, a long-time enemy.

Although Congress provided money and troops to remove the Five Civilized Tribes, it offered no plan for helping them to resettle and adjust to their new environs. Such aid usually came from volunteers sponsored by church groups: Catholics, Baptists, Methodists, and others set up missions and schools to teach the

Although the U.S. government promised money and supplies to resettled Indians, it rarely followed through on its promises. Here, a nineteenth-century cartoon illustrates this by showing a government official handing out holey blankets and rotten meat to waiting Indians.

displaced Indians the Christian faith, basic literacy, and manual arts.

Although the government promised to provide Indians with guns, plows, seed, kettles, traps, blankets, and such, these articles did not arrive in full measure, or at all, for years. Often, corrupt government officials, military leaders, and even tribal chiefs confiscated the supplies for personal profit.

Food allotments from the government were also dangerously scant. Daily rations consisted only of meat, bread, and salt.

Despite being overwhelmed by shock, misery, fear, and heartbreak, many dislocated Indians tried their best to farm, to hunt nearby buffalo, and to build new communities. As bad as their lives now were, wrote Foreman, "The one ray of light and hope was the conviction that at least they were so far removed from the white man that they could look forward to a life free from his devastating blight."[66]

The Indians were wrong. They were not safe. A new wave of whites, who had every intention of taking away these lands too, was headed their way.

Immigration Pressures

During the years of forced removal of the Five Civilized Tribes, a half-million Europeans immigrated to the United States and settled in Indiana, Ohio, Michigan, and Illinois, increasing the public appetite for land. In 1837 the nation reeled from a widespread economic crisis that resulted in loss of jobs for thousands of northern factory workers. At the same time, many poor farmers in the South went bankrupt and were forced to sell their small farms. Large numbers of these displaced Americans joined the flood of immigrants who sought new lands and opportunities in the West.

By the early 1840s, this westerly quest had developed into a burning nationwide obsession, fueled by a popular belief called Manifest [plainly obvious] Destiny. According to this notion, Americans had a "divine mission" to expand to the Pacific, perhaps even across the entire continent, including Canada and Mexico. Politicians, editors, scholars, preachers, and business leaders all urged their fellow Americans to seek their fortunes in the West and fulfill America's destiny.

Lust for land only partly explained why Manifest Destiny became such a popular idea. By this time many Americans firmly believed that American democracy was superior to all other forms of government. Territorial expansion seemed a justifiable way of spreading the idea of representative government.

John Louis O'Sullivan, editor of the *New York Morning News,* explained it as follows:

> Our manifest destiny [is] to overspread and to possess the whole of the continent which Providence [God] has given us for the development of the great experiment of liberty and federated self-government entrusted to us.[67]

Powerful business figures who dreamed of building major American seaports on the Pacific coast to increase trade with Asia saw Manifest Destiny as a driving force that could make their wishes come true. Meanwhile, some Americans argued that the United States had to expand to the limits of the continent to keep foreign countries from gaining a foothold on North America and posing a threat to the nation. After all, they pointed out, the troublesome British still possessed territory in the far Northwest.

Through all their fuss and furor, however, the champions of Manifest Destiny showed little concern for the rights of other human beings—Native Americans and Mexicans—who already lived on the lands in question.

Oregon Lands Open to Settlers

In the early 1830s, only a scattering of Americans—fur trappers, miners, and explorers—lived in the far Northwest Territory

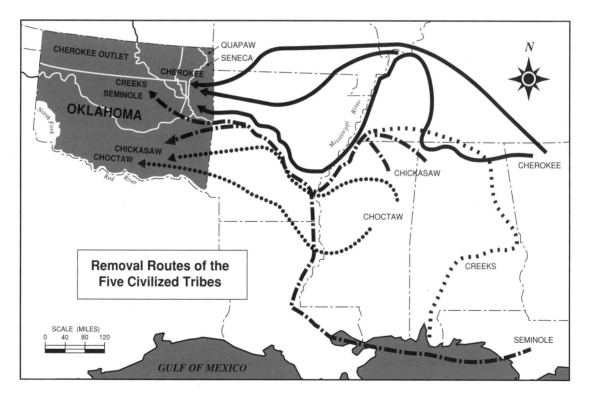

Removal Routes of the Five Civilized Tribes

SCALE (MILES)
0 40 80 120

Initially, white settlers tried to cross the Great Plains as quickly as possible, believing the lands to be uninhabitable.

called Oregon. But the area's population began to grow after 1833 when glowing descriptions of the region appeared in the eastern press.

Land-hungry settlers from the Mississippi Valley and elsewhere packed their belongings in wagons and headed west along the Oregon Trail, a wagon road that ranged two thousand miles from Independence, Missouri, through the Rockies to the Willamette Valley in Oregon. By 1846 five thousand settlers had made the trip.

Coming fast behind them were thousands of others fleeing religious persecution in the East; they were Mormons, who would end their trek by carving out a religious refuge in Utah Territory.

At first, few of America's westward bound pioneers regarded the vast prairies—the Great Plains of the Midwest—as desirable places for homesteads. Most pioneers wanted to cross as quickly as possible the area they nicknamed the "Great American Desert," because it was arid, almost treeless, and hard to plow.

Not many years later, others realized that these lands were actually among the most fertile fields in the world. For the time being, though, the focus was on the Far West. And to reach America's extreme western regions, many emigrants first had to cross Indian Territory.

With growing alarm, Native Americans kept vigil on an ever-growing number of wagons, horses, oxen, and dogs trespassing on their lands.

Texas to the Pacific

Author Dee Brown sets the stage for the next act:

> Scarcely were the refugees settled behind the security of the "permanent Indian frontier" when white soldiers began marching westward through the Indian country. The white men of the United States . . . were marching to war with the white men who had conquered the Indians of Mexico.[68]

Ever since 1821, many Americans had migrated to Texas—then a province of

A wagon trail of settlers moves west along the Oregon Trail. While passing through Indian territory, many whites killed buffalo, trampled Indian pastureland, and killed Indians.

Mexico, which had recently won its independence from Spain.

After the United States defeated Mexico in a war over boundary disputes in 1848, many more Americans relocated to the area. The United States ended up with two-fifths of Mexico—a vast area stretching from Texas to California opened to American settlers. "All of it," observes Dee Brown, "was west of the 'permanent Indian frontier.'"[69]

The United States added even more land in 1853, when Mexico sold to its neighbor above the Rio Grande the strip of territory that today makes up the southern stretch of Arizona and New Mexico.

Now the United States could proudly claim ownership of contiguous territory from the Atlantic all the way to the Pacific. For Native Americans, this achievement brought great alarm: The Indian Territory was now dangerously sandwiched between two huge territories belonging to the land-hungry United States.

California Gold

Another stampede of settlers to the Far West began in 1848, when gold was discovered at Sutter's Mill in northern California. News of the discovery flashed around the globe. So many people fell prey to gold's hypnotic spell that by the end of 1849 California's population had swollen from twenty thousand to nearly five times

A new wave of settlers moved west once gold was discovered in California.

that number. Miners, prospectors, and opportunists of all sorts from around the world rushed to the Sierra Nevada, hoping to find great wealth. Some adventurers took the long way around South America to California; others slogged through the jungles of Nicaragua. Many more, however, crossed Indian Territory in endless wagon trains to reach the promised land.

Whatever the reason whites had for penetrating Indian lands, the same pattern of behavior emerged: Migrants wantonly killed buffalo, trampled pastureland, spread disease, and shot Indians.

Tension Mounts

Many whites decided to stay on Indian lands and, once again, sounded an old refrain: Indians were savages who were not fit to be stewards of the lands they possessed; only whites were able to fill this role.

In 1850 an editor for a Kansas newspaper wrote what many westerners believed. Indians were

> a set of miserable, dirty, lousy, blanketed, thieving, lying, sneaking, murdering, graceless, faithless, gut-eating skunks as the Lord ever permitted to infect the earth, and whose immediate extermination all men, except Indian agents and traders, should pray for.[70]

A Conference at Fort Laramie

When tensions between Indians and whites neared the breaking point, the United States sponsored a huge conference in September 1851 at Fort Laramie, a military outpost in Wyoming manned by federal troops to protect the Oregon Trail.

An estimated ten thousand men, women, and children from many tribes and bands—Cheyenne, Arapaho, Sioux, Crow, Assiniboine, Arikara, Atsina—arrived on horseback and on foot, dressed in full tribal regalia to work out treaties with the United States. The conference, which was the biggest single meeting of Indians in history, was a success. Tribal representatives devised boundaries acceptable to themselves and promised white agents not to molest pioneers on the Oregon Trail. The Indians also acknowledged that the United States had a right to maintain the trail and erect army forts to protect it.

In return, the United States agreed to pay the Indians $50,000 a year for the next fifty years in the form of food, supplies, domesticated animals, and tools. Later the Senate (which approves all treaties) reduced the number of years to ten.

Massive Migration into Indian Territory

The federal government made a similar agreement with the Comanches and Kiowas at Fort Atkinson on the Arkansas River (in present-day Kansas): Indians were to receive goods for ten years, and the United States could build and protect roads for emigrants, notably the Santa Fe Trail, an eight-hundred-mile thoroughfare from Independence, Missouri, to Santa Fe, New Mexico.

Despite the good intentions represented by the pacts of Fort Laramie and Fort Atkinson, peace on the Great Plains was doomed by the sheer massive number of whites who trespassed on Indian territory. In *The Long Death,* Ralph K. Andrist writes:

> The permanent Indian country was dying fast. Already the frontier that was to have divided it forever from the white man's world had bulged and given way along a great section under pressure from land-hungry settlers. The myths about the worthlessness of grasslands [the Great Plains] were evaporating; pioneers had learned that tall-grass prairie land, at least, was tremendously fertile. The

Indians had been pushed off almost all the prairie land of Minnesota and Iowa—part of the original permanent Indian Country—by the weary method of land cession treaties, and bigger things were ahead.[71]

In the early 1850s, Americans increased their demands on the federal government to open up Indian lands. Among them were businessmen who planned to build a transcontinental railroad through Indian lands that would lead to the Pacific coast.

As the government went to work on the Plains tribes, it also imposed treaties on Indians in the Far West to give up 157 million acres in Idaho, Oregon, and Washington.

Splitting Nebraska

As whites moved west, they carried along a bitter and hostile debate that was tearing up the nation, the issue of slavery. A new aspect of the argument developed: Should slavery be allowed in the federal territories?

In 1854, in an attempt to please everyone except slaves and Indians, Sen. Stephen A. Douglas of Illinois, chairman of the Committee on the Territories, pushed a bill through Congress that split the Nebraska Territory into two parts: Nebraska in the north, Kansas in the south. Settlers in each area would decide for their respective territories the issues of statehood [whether to join the Union] and slavery [whether the practice should be allowed]. The Indians residing in those parts received no voice in determining who would live on their lands.

To clear the way for immigrants into Nebraska, the government made treaties with many tribes—the Omaha, Ottoe, Missouria, Sac and Fox, Iowa, Kickapoo, Delaware, Shawnee, Kaskaskia, Peoria, Wea, Piankashaw, and Miami—who gave up 13 million acres, and retained about 1.3 million acres for themselves.

Some tribes exchanged their land for money. Others received nothing. Although many Indians were furious about the concessions, they agreed to them in the belief that at long last their homelands would be "permanently fixed." Ralph K. Andrist writes:

> Only the land belonging to the Five Civilized Tribes in Oklahoma still remained without any organized state or territorial government. It was considered quite certain that this land, which was soon labeled the Indian Territory, was too worthless ever to be wanted by white men, and that the Indians living there could possess it indefinitely without being molested.[72]

Whites, however, did want this land. Therefore settlers molested Indians in the newly created territories of Kansas and Nebraska, attempting to drive them out. They even encroached onto the cramped Indian reservations, violating all treaties and ignoring Indian protests. George W. Manypenny, commissioner of Indian Affairs, stated in his annual report for 1854:

> Already the white population is occupying the lands between and adjacent to the Indian reservations, and even going west of and beyond them, and at no distant day, all the country immediately to the west of the reserves, which is worth occupying, will have been taken up.[73]

So far, emigrants had been swarming in from the East. But in his report, Manypenny also noted the arrival of a new wave of settlers from the West, a human tide that "comes sweeping like an avalanche from the Pacific coast, almost overwhelming the indigenous Indians in its approaches."[74]

Tribal Conflicts in Indian Territory

In The Five Civilized Tribes, *Grant Foreman quotes an 1834 document from the Office of Indian Affairs containing this excerpt of a letter from Creek chiefs complaining about marauding Delawares.*

"Large hordes of them [Delawares] are said to be within and on the borders of the Creek country, killing and destroying the game; and destroying the cane and pastures; and at this time there are large encampments of them on the Seminole land. They have immense droves of horses pasturing on the cane, killing up all the deer, bear and turkeys, and destroying the Buffaloe that came in or near the Creek country, killing hundreds of them for their skins and tongues, stealing horses from the neighboring tribes and bringing them to the Creek country, by which means the Creeks apprehend being brought into collision [anticipate fights] with their neighbors; and they therefore claim the protection of Government from these troublesome people."

In spite of agreements that preserved Indian rights to land, white settlers continuously violated such agreements, passing through Indian land at will. Indians became increasingly upset by this behavior. Here, an Indian chief forbids a wagon train from crossing through his territory.

Manypenny witnessed a shameless land theft in 1854 when white speculators and settlers began building the city of Leavenworth on Delaware lands. Officers of the U.S. Army—military men who were empowered to protect Indians from such encroachment—merely watched the illegal activity; they did nothing to stop it. Wrote Manypenny in 1856:

Trespasses and depredations of every conceivable kind have been committed on the Indians. They have been personally maltreated, their property stolen, their timber destroyed, their possessions encroached upon, and divers [various] other wrongs and injuries done them.[75]

Despite the urgent protests from Commissioner Manypenny and other men of conscience, the federal government refused to stop the land-grabbing settlers.

"They [the Indians] are in abject want of food half the year," Thomas Fitzgerald, an Indian agent in the Indian Territory wrote in his 1854 report, "[and] different tribes are forced to contend with hostile nations in support for their villages. Their women are pinched with want and their children are constantly crying with hunger.[76]

And it was hunger that finally broke a strained and uneasy peace on the plains.

Armed Conflict Arises

Four years after the Fort Laramie Conference a minor argument triggered a bloody and brutal cycle of revenge killing between the Plains Indians and whites.

One day in 1854 near Fort Laramie, a famished young Sioux came across a sickly stray cow in the wilderness and killed it for food. Later, the animal's owner, a Mormon emigrant, demanded reparations of $25. A Sioux leader offered $10, which the owner refused.

The following day, a detail of thirty soldiers led by a rash and foolish young lieutenant named John L. Grattan, descended on a nearby Sioux encampment and demanded that the Indians either pay $25 or surrender the youth. When the Indians angrily balked, Grattan's soldiers opened fire, killing several Sioux and wounding many others.

Instantly the surviving Indians rushed the soldiers and killed all but one man, who managed to make his way back to the fort to relate what had happened.

Then began a years-long series of bloody attacks and reprisals in which both Indians and whites committed horrible and senseless atrocities.

Civil War Dawns

In 1861 the outbreak of the American Civil War temporarily slowed incoming tides of whites. Indians were amazed that whites were now more intent on killing each other than them.

Like the rest of America, white westerners divided into Confederate and Union forces and fought each other from California to Texas to the Indian Territory. Blue-coated troops even abandoned army forts in the West to pursue Confederate sympathizers, leaving settlers more unprotected against Indian attacks than ever before.

During this period, Indian leaders across the West urged their tribes to take advantage of this division between whites and drive the interlopers out of Indian land forever.

Chapter

6 Revolts, Removals, and Reservations

Among the first to revolt were the Sioux in Minnesota. A disturbing history of encroaching settlers, broken treaties, and swindling traders had reduced these Plains Indians to living in misery, hunger, and smoldering resentment on a reservation 10 miles long and 150 miles wide—a fraction of the vast territory they had once roamed.

Often the Sioux's "annuity"—in the form of food and supplies from the U.S. government—arrived late at the federally run Indian agency on the Yellow Medicine River, forcing the Sioux to beg for credit from white traders to avoid starving. While some whites sympathized with the Indians,

others hardened against them. "So far as I am concerned, if they are hungry let them eat grass," remarked Indian trader Andrew Myrick.[77]

Tensions snapped on August 17, 1862. That afternoon four hungry Sioux braves returned from an unsuccessful hunt, fell into an argument, and goaded each other into killing four white settlers. News of the senseless slaughter terrified whites across the prairie.

Many Sioux, fearing white retaliation, hurriedly moved their families away from the region. Others, though, were in the mood for war. Under the command of a

Fed up with the U.S. government's failure to provide annuities and supplies, desperately hungry and poor Sioux began an uprising against white settlers.

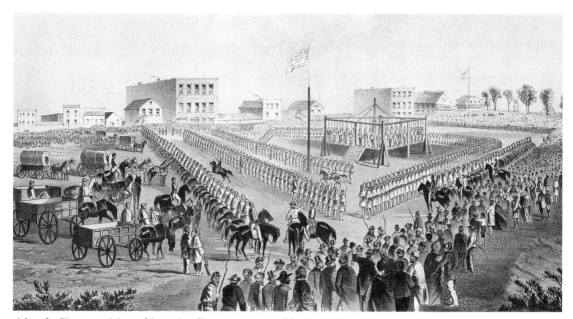

After the Sioux uprising, thirty-nine Sioux are executed by the U.S. government for their role in killing whites.

leader named Little Crow, thirteen hundred warriors launched a full-scale war against white settlers in the Minnesota River valley. Warriors rampaged and massacred young and old, men and women, burning hundreds of buildings and destroying crops. After one of the early massacres, the body of Andrew Myrick was found; a wad of prairie grass stuffed into his mouth.

Alarmed, the Minnesota state government responded to the emergency by authorizing Col. Henry Hastings Sibley to lead an army of volunteers to the troubled area. The Sioux had killed more than four hundred whites by the time Sibley's men had quelled the uprising.

Of the 392 warriors caught and later tried in white courts, 303 were sentenced to death. But a full-scale mass execution never took place. Episcopal Rev. H. B. Whipple of Minnesota, a renowned advocate of Indian policy reform, pleaded suc-

cessfully with President Abraham Lincoln to spare the lives of many of the warriors. Only 39 were hanged; the others served long prison sentences.

As many Sioux had feared, white retaliation was harsh. In 1863, for example, Congress severely punished the Sioux by taking all their Minnesota lands and forcing the Indians into Dakota Territory. Many settlers, perhaps deliberately, mistook even the peaceful Winnebago Indians as their enemies, and shot them when they left the reservation. Instead of protecting the Winnebago, however, the federal government forced them to pay for their own removal to another reservation two thousand miles away in Missouri. Here, adequate supplies from the U.S. government did not arrive on time, causing many Indians to starve. Others were murdered and raped by marauding whites.

Whites' thirst for Indian land was never slaked. Wherever Indians settled, even when it was within the guidelines set up by the U.S. government, they were inevitably forced to relocate.

Forced Removal in the Southwest

In the Southwest, whites cracked down on bands of Apaches, who relied on raiding and stealing from Americans, Mexicans, and other Indians to survive in the mercilessly hot, arid climate. Ever since their arrival in the region during the 1850s, in fact, white settlers had suffered raids of warlike Apaches. Among the most feared was the Mescalero band.

But during the early days of the American Civil War, the raiding days of these Indians came to an end. In New Mexico, Gen. James Carleton, a Union officer, had troops at his disposal but no gray-coated Confederates to fight. He decided to put his men to work by rounding up Mescaleros. "There is to be no council with the Indians, nor any talks," Carleton ordered. "The men are to be slain whenever and wherever they can be found. The women and children may be taken as prisoners, but, of course they are not to be killed."[78]

Fully aware that Carleton's forces were more numerous and better armed, the Mescaleros surrendered and accepted relocation to a forty-square-mile reservation called Bosque Redondo (Spanish for Round Grove), a barren wasteland along the Pecos River in central New Mexico.

Carleton's work, however, was not finished. He and his supporters decided to remove all Indians in the Rio Grande valley to open the region to homesteaders. Next on the removal list were the Navajos. Carleton ordered these pueblo-dwelling people moved to Bosque Redondo by July 20, 1862. Those who refused would be hunted down and driven out.

The Navajos were not intimidated. "I will not go to the Bosque," replied Navajo leader Barboncito at a meeting with Carleton. "I will never leave my country, not even if it means I will be killed."[79]

The midsummer deadline arrived and not one Navajo appeared for deportation. Infuriated, Carleton hired famed Indian fighter Kit Carson to lead an expedition to track down and capture all Navajos. A bloody six-month campaign ensued, during which white soldiers killed Navajos, burned homes, and destroyed fruit trees, crops, and livestock. The final blow came in winter, when Carson's soldiers trapped freezing Navajos in a steep, rocky canyon, where the Indians surrendered.

During the spring, more than fourteen hundred men, women, and children were forced at gunpoint to begin the first of several "Long Walks" to Bosque Redondo. Eventually, more than five thousand Navajos made the three-hundred-mile trip. Hundreds died along the way. Many children were kidnapped, perhaps by some of Carleton's men, and sold into slavery.

"The Navahos had the fortitude to bear freezing weather, hunger, dysentery, jeers of the soldiers, and the hard three-hundred-mile journey," writes Dee Brown, "but they could not bear the homesickness, the loss of their land."[80]

Bosque Redondo was a horrid place. Conditions were unsanitary, drinking water filthy. The land was not fit for farming. Moreover, Navajos were crowded together with their ancient enemies—the Mescalero Apaches. Because there was not adequate shelter, many Indians had to burrow into the sand like animals to avoid the dangers of exposure.

Heartbroken, sick, and dying, Native Americans had no choice but to rely on their white captors to stay alive. But the fort did not have enough good food, clothing, medicine, and other supplies for its ill and starving inmates. Hundreds of Indians died. When desperate Navajos began to leave the disease-ridden concentration camp without permission, Carleton ordered his troops to shoot to kill.

Alarmed white officials at the reservation eventually notified Congress of the squalid conditions at Bosque Redondo, and the federal government launched an official investigation. As a result, Carleton's relocation effort was declared a disaster, and the general was reprimanded and reassigned elsewhere.

Then in an uncommon move in the history of the West, the federal government released some seven thousand Navajos and on June 1, 1868, allowed them to return to another reservation near their beloved native lands.

Indian fighter Kit Carson was hired to track down remaining Navajo and either kill them or force them to relocate to the intolerable Bosque Redondo.

In 1866 A. B. Norton, a new superintendent, arrived at Bosque Redondo and was appalled at the conditions he found. His reaction, excerpted in Dee Brown's Bury My Heart at Wounded Knee, *contains this passage.*

"The sooner it [Bosque Redondo] is abandoned and the Indians removed, the better. . . . Do you expect an Indian to be satisfied and contented deprived of the common comforts of life, without which a white man would not be contented anywhere? Would any sensible man select a spot for a reservation for 8,000 Indians where the water is scarcely bearable, where the soil is poor and cold, and where the muskite [mesquite] roots 12 miles distant are the only wood for the Indians to use?. . .

If they remain on this reservation they must always be held there by force, and not from choice. O! let them go back, or take them to where they can have good cool water to drink, wood plenty to keep them from freezing to death, and where the soil will produce something for them to eat."

Sand Creek: The Chivington Massacre

Conflict over land was also taking a turn for the worse in Colorado, where whites swarmed onto Cheyenne and Arapaho lands, in clear violation of the Fort Laramie treaty. At first, Indians tried to live in peace with the newcomers, who had been arriving in great numbers since 1858, when gold was discovered near Pikes Peak, Colorado. Relations became tense, however, as whites began to take over the region.

In 1861 the U.S. government, disregarding Indian territorial rights, officially created the Colorado Territory. Next, it appointed a governor and persuaded Cheyenne and Arapaho tribal leaders to cede their lands to the United States and accept a small reservation in southeastern Colorado, located between the Arkansas River and Sand Creek.

From its onset, the treaty generated bitter controversy. Whites expected the Indians to stay within the boundaries of the reservation at all times. But the Cheyenne believed the treaty restrictions applied only to the location of villages. Since the reservation consisted mostly of worthless land and lacked sufficient game, Indian hunters wandered beyond the reservation boundaries to hunt.

At first, Cheyenne hunting parties avoided white settlers and soldiers whenever possible. But eventually clashes occurred. Most of the fighting was episodic, but when Arapahos killed and butchered a family of four in Denver, Colorado, in August 1864, Colorado's governor John Evans placed a former preacher, John Chivington, in command of a volunteer state militia charged with quelling Indian violence.

Chivington's troops first raided Cheyenne camps in northern Colorado. Next, on May 16, they attacked a hunting party in Kansas. Among those slain was Chief Lean Bear, a tribal leader who proudly wore a medal given him by President Abraham Lincoln.

Cheyenne Revenge

Chivington's actions provoked the Dog Soldiers, the elite Cheyenne warrior class, to visit revenge against all whites. Writer Irving Stone tells how this was accomplished: "The Indians made swift attacks on stages [stagecoaches], mail coaches, freight trains, paralyzing passenger and food supply lines, earning Colorado the reputation as the most dangerous area in the United States to settle."[81]

Yielding to a frightened public, Governor Evans called on all Colorado citizens "to be good patriots and kill all hostile Indians."[82] However, he also urged friendly tribes to report to Fort Lyon in southwestern Colorado, where they would be fed and protected.

Although bloody fighting continued, two Indian leaders—Chief Black Kettle of the Cheyenne and the Arapahos' White Antelope—met with Evans, Chivington, and other whites in Denver to seek peaceful solutions. Chivington was blunt about his own terms: "My rule of fighting . . . Indians is to fight them until they lay down their arms and submit."[83]

Despite Chivington's harsh demands, Indian leaders left the meeting satisfied that the talks had gone well and convinced that peace would soon come. But white officials saw things differently. Governor Evans, in fact, was distressed. He had recently formed a new regiment that was itching to see combat. "What shall I do with the third regiment if I make peace?" he asked one of his officers. "[They were] . . . raised [they signed up] to kill Indians and they must kill Indians."[84]

Elsewhere, a higher military authority also opposed an armistice. "I want no peace till the Indians suffer more," wrote Maj. Gen. Samuel R. Curtis from Fort Leavenworth.[85]

Bands of Arapaho and Cheyenne, seeking to comply with Evans's instructions, arrived at Fort Lyon on November 9, 1864. Here, base commander Maj. Scott J. Anthony ordered the Indians to camp along the banks of nearby Sand Creek and promised them military protection. But no protection was ever given.

During the early dawn of November 28, Colonel Chivington, disdaining Anthony's promise, led a surprise attack against the sleeping Indians at Sand Creek. He gave the order of the day: "Kill and scalp all, big and little; nits make lice."[86]

The soldiers took the camp by surprise, firing rifles and cannons at terrified Indian men and women, children and infants. During the onslaught, White Antelope walked calmly toward the attackers, his arms raised in a gesture of peace. He was shot to death. Black Kettle hoisted both an American flag and a white banner of surrender. Still came the deadly rain of bullets.

Not content to murder the peaceful Indians, Chivington's men committed individual acts of savagery. They mutilated the bodies of slain Indians, cutting off private parts of females and lifting bloody scalps to

A drawing shows the attack against bands of Arapaho and Cheyenne camped at Sand Creek. The attack would later be called the Chivington Massacre, as white soldiers savagely slaughtered and mutilated women, children, and elderly men.

take them home as souvenirs. By that afternoon, 105 Indians lay dead and butchered.

Afterward, Chivington and his men were hailed as heroes in Denver. "All acquitted themselves well," read the *Denver News*. "Colorado soldiers have again covered themselves with glory."[87] At a local theater, Chivington exhibited a hundred scalps and regaled audiences with tales of slaughter.

Nationwide, however, an angry and aroused public reviled Chivington. A military commission investigated the carnage, relieved Chivington of his command, and condemned his actions. However, no criminal charges were brought against the state militia leader.

American Indians were less forgiving. Author Irving Stone reports:

> By his action the intrepid Colonel Chivington united all Indians in Colorado, not only the remaining plains tribes but the Sioux, Comanche, Apaches, Kiowas, and . . . Utes . . . . The winter of 1864–1865 was for Colorado an unrelenting reign of terror, the Indians de-

stroying everything they could lay their hands on: telegraph lines, ranches, warehouses, devastating every mile of stage route . . . , attacking and killing soldiers at isolated forts.[88]

Trouble to the North

Within a year, the Cheyennes and Arapahos wearied of fighting and called off their raids. But as Colorado quieted, trouble flared when whites flocked to the northwestern lands of the Sioux in Montana and Wyoming, feverishly searching for gold. To accommodate the prospectors, the federal government planned to build a road and a series of forts along the Powder River to connect the mining towns of Bozeman, Montana, and Virginia City, Nevada, with the East.

These plans were stymied by a band of Teton Sioux led by Chief Red Cloud, who refused to grant access through Indian

This passage from a scathing report from an 1865 congressional committee concerning Colonel Chivington's massacre of Cheyenne Indians appears in Wexler's Western Expansion.

"As to Colonel Chivington, your committee can hardly find fitting terms to describe his conduct. Wearing the uniform of the United States, which should be the emblem of justice and humanity; holding the important position of commander of a military district, and therefore having the honor of the government to that extent in his keeping, he deliberately planned and executed a foul and dastardly massacre which would have disgraced the veriest savage among those who were the victims of his cruelty."

Chief Red Cloud refused to allow the U.S. government to build a road through Indian land and led warriors against the U.S. Army in 1866.

lands. When the government began the project anyway, Red Cloud and three thousand warriors went on the warpath during the summer of 1866. A wave of shock swept through the nation when Americans learned that the Sioux had ambushed, killed, and mutilated the bodies of Capt. William J. Fetterman and eighty-two troops along the Powder River. The so-called Bozeman Trail was never completed.

The Peace Commission

By now the American public was deeply disturbed by the bloodshed in the West. The massacres at Sand Creek and Powder River, plus numerous other Indian uprisings, forced Congress to rethink its Indian policy. In Washington, political leaders clashed over what to do next. Westerners and conservatives demanded a harsh military crackdown on the warring tribes. Some called for even sterner measures.

"We have come to this point in the history of the country that there is no place beyond population to which you can remove the Indian," thundered Maine's Senator Lot M. Morrill, "and the precise question is: Will you exterminate him or will you fix an abiding place for him?"[89]

In the end, other voices, mostly those of easterners, prevailed, successfully urging Congress to adopt a "humane" treatment of Indians. In 1867 the lawmakers instructed a "Peace Commission" to negotiate with western Indian leaders to "remove the causes of war; secure the frontier settlements and railroad construction; and establish a system for civilizing the tribes."[90]

A further goal was to force Indians to move to "small reservations" rather than to allow them to dwell "concentrated" on larger ones. Peace commissioners also offered Indians protection, food, and supplies if they submitted to U.S. authority and relocated in two major regions.

Critics, including Bishop Whipple of Minnesota, claimed that "the peace policy was little more than a name. No change was made in the Indian system; no rights of property were given; no laws were passed to protect Indians."[91]

In the fall of 1867, leaders of the Cheyenne, Arapaho, Kiowa, and Comanche tribes parleyed with federal peace commissioners at Medicine Lodge Creek in southern Kansas. Whites wanted all the tribes removed from their homelands, to make way for the construction of a railroad along the Smoky River in Kansas. Indians sought peaceful coexistence and the right to remain on their lands. Finally the Indians reluctantly agreed to sign treaties ceding their lands along the Arkansas and Canadian Rivers in Indian Territory. They also promised to abandon their nomadic ways and relocate on a reservation between the Red and Washita Rivers in western Indian Territory.

At Fort Laramie in 1868, the members of the Peace Commission also struck an agreement with the rebellious Sioux; the government promised it would cease building the Bozeman Trail if the Sioux of Wyoming and Montana agreed to stop their raids and relocate to the Black Hills of the Dakotas. Here, on their most sacred

Arapaho and Comanche sign a treaty with federal peace commissioners in 1867. Tired of the endless fighting, U.S. citizens wanted the Indian problem solved once and for all.

William Sherman signs a peace treaty with the Sioux at Fort Laramie in 1868. The United States promised land concessions and supplies to cooperative Indians.

lands, they were to receive food and supplies from the government and instruction on how to become farmers and Christians.

Federal negotiators once again promised that no whites would be allowed on Indian lands. Such a promise, as usual, proved impossible to keep.

Punishing the Five Civilized Tribes

The federal government by now had decided on a place for the removed southern Plains tribes: lands that belonged to other Indians.

During the Civil War, many individual members of the Five Civilized Tribes had sided with the Confederacy, whose leaders had offered them more freedom than they would have obtained from the Union. The Confederates also promised never to absorb the Indians into a territory or state. Finally, many Indians sympathized with the southern cause because they, like many southerners, owned slaves.

But the Indians chose unwisely; Union victory in 1865 brought punishment to the Indians for their apparent disloyalty. Soured by war, the federal government retaliated by pressuring the Five Civilized Tribes into ceding the western half of their territories. These lands then became the new resettlement area for the southern Cheyenne, Arapaho, Kiowa, Comanche, and Kiowa–Apache.

Non-Treaty Bands Resist

Many Indians refused to cooperate with the Peace Commission. The "non-treaty bands" of Sioux, Arapaho, and Cheyenne feared an end to their nomadic way of life and continued attacking whites across the plains from Texas to Kansas.

The federal government responded in 1867 by putting a powerful figure in

U.S. troops ignore earlier promises and gun down peaceful Cheyenne at the Washita River. Historians argue about massacres such as this one, believing that the U.S. goal became complete annihilation, not appeasement, with the Indian tribes.

command of federal troops in the West: William Tecumseh Sherman—the Union general who had helped smash the South during the Civil War.

Sherman's strategy was far different from that of the Peace Commission. "The more [Indians] we can kill this year," he said, "the less will have to be killed in the next war. . . . They all have to be killed or be maintained as a species of paupers [poor people]."[92]

One of the most zealous of Indian fighters under Sherman's command was the rambunctious Lt. Col. George Armstrong Custer, a man the Indians called "Yellow Hair." This arrogant and flamboyant officer repeatedly proved himself capable of slaughtering Indians, hostile or peaceful.

Custer's lethal power became clear during the autumn of 1868. At the time, Black Kettle and other survivors of the Chivington Massacre were trying to live peacefully with other Cheyenne in western Indian Territory on the upper Washita River. Worried that they could become innocent vic-

tims during this army campaign to crack down on hostile Indians, they approached the commander of the Indian Territory, General Hazen, and asked for protection. The officer was moved by Black Kettle's sincere desire for peace and promised the Cheyenne the protection of his troops.

Meanwhile, Yellow Hair, an old rival of Hazen's, was making different plans for Black Kettle's band. Custer disregarded his fellow officer's promise to Black Kettle and ordered the Seventh Cavalry to attack the Cheyenne on the dawn of November 7, 1868.

Horror-struck, Black Kettle and his wife awoke to the realization that the unspeakable nightmare of Sand Creek was being repeated. They tried to escape, but like everyone else that bloody morning, fell dead in a storm of American bullets. When the killing stopped, 103 Cheyenne, mostly women and children, lay dead along the Washita River.

By such bloody means, the army quelled the West.

7 The Final Stand

Although Congress never officially declared war on American Indians, there were more than two hundred armed conflicts between Indians and whites between 1869 and 1874. According to S. L. A. Marshall, author of *Crimsoned Prairie*:

> Violence beset the western frontier and lasted and lasted because the fundamental interests of the two sides were so wholly irreconcilable as to leave little or no room for compromise. Due to the absence of any middle ground, there occurred intolerable grievances to white man and red. When these basic conditions are present, war or revolution becomes inevitable.[93]

Time after time, Indians lost ground in these conflicts. Indeed, as 1874 drew to a close, many Americans concluded that Indian power across the entire West was broken once and for all.

In Oregon, for example, the U.S. cavalry brutally punished the Modoc Indians for leaving their reservation at Klamath. Between 1848 and 1870, miners and military and citizen–vigilante groups killed between fifty and seventy thousand Indians in California and forced the survivors from their lands. When Comanche and Kiowa warriors surrendered at Fort Sill, Oklahoma, Indian resistance vanished on the northern plains of Texas.

After almost four hundred years of effort, when whites were close to total domination of North America's native peoples, some bemoaned the tragic outcome. "Greed and avarice on the part of the whites—in other words, the almighty dollar," asserted experienced Indian fighter Gen. George Crook, "is at the bottom of nine-tenths of all our Indian troubles."[94]

But the white conquest of American Indians was not yet finished. More blood was yet to be shed.

Little Bighorn

By the summer of 1874, George Custer, who now held the rank of general, led more than twelve hundred men on an expedition into the Black Hills of western Dakota—the sacred lands of the Sioux, which were forbidden to whites by treaty.

Officially, Custer and his men had trespassed on Sioux lands for purposes of exploration, but soon they found what they really had hoped to find: gold. News of their discovery spread fast. An editorial in the Chicago *Inter Ocean* announced:

Cavalry commanded by Custer cross the plains of Dakota Territory. Once gold was found in the Black Hills of South Dakota, Indians found themselves once again faced with thousands of white settlers determined to encroach upon their land.

There is gold in the hills and rivers of the region, and the white man desires to take possession of it. . . . [The Indians] must decrease [so] that the newcomers may grow in wealth. Happy for him the day when the last of the tribes shall fold his blankets around his shrunken limbs, and take his final sleep, to waken in the eyes of the Great Spirit.[95]

The 1868 Fort Laramie treaty had promised the Sioux that no unauthorized persons without Indian permission "shall ever be permitted to pass over, settle upon, or reside in the territory."[96] The meaning of these words is unmistakable. But when miners, settlers, and opportunists of all sorts swarmed into the Black Hills, the government did little to oust them. Instead, it offered to buy the lands.

The Sioux scorned the offer. Infuriated over the arrival of whites, as many as three thousand Sioux and Cheyenne warriors—the largest group of Indian fighting forces ever assembled—gathered in Montana and prepared for the warpath.

In December 1875 federal government officials recognized that the massing of hostile Indians represented a growing danger to whites. They ordered all Indians to vacate their settlements in the Black Hills of Dakota and Wyoming territories and move to reservations or face military reprisals.

The defiant Indians remained and prepared to wage battle. In the spring of 1876 the army responded by sending into Montana three large regiments, each moving from a different direction, with instructions to converge on the Indians.

Low Dog Speaks of Custer's Last Stand

As quoted in Story of the Great American West, *edited by Edward S. Barnard, Low Dog, a chief of the Oglala Sioux, gave the Leavenworth* Weekly Times *this account of Custer's last stand, which appeared in the Kansas newspaper on August 18, 1881.*

"They came on us like a thunderbolt. I never before nor since saw men so brave and fearless as those white warriors. We retreated until our men got all together, and then we charged upon them. I called to my men, 'This is a good day to die: follow me.' We massed our men, and that no man should fall back, every man whipped another man's horse and we rushed right upon them. . . . The white warriors dismounted to fire. . . . They held their horses' reins on one arm while they were shooting, but their horses were so frightened that they pulled the men all around, and a great many of their shots went up in the air. . . . I did not see Gen. Custer. . . . We did not know . . . that he was the white chief."

Custer, vastly outnumbered, is surrounded and killed by his lifelong enemies.

On the morning of June 25, 1876, General Custer's Seventh Cavalry, made up of six hundred exhausted men, arrived deep in Sioux Territory near a large Indian encampment along the Little Bighorn River. Custer's orders required him to await reinforcements before attacking, but Yellow Hair desired all the glory of an Indian victory for himself. Accordingly, he divided the Seventh Cavalry into three groups and sent two of them to attack what he thought were minor Sioux camps along the Little Bighorn.

Members of the U.S. cavalry pursue hostile Indians. Many Indians refused to peacefully relocate to uninhabitable reservations.

Custer was wrong. What his men rushed into was a major Indian stronghold. More than 2,500 Sioux, led by Chiefs Sitting Bull, Crazy Horse, and Rain-in-the-Face, and 8,000 to 10,000 other warriors from various other tribes descended on Custer and his troops.

In less than a half-hour, Yellow Hair and 225 soldiers—about one-third of his regiment—lay dead. Across the West, Indians cheered the news of Custer's death.

Their euphoria, however, was short-lived.

The Death of Indian Power on the Northern Plains

The timing of Custer's last stand, as the Battle of Little Bighorn came to be called, proved disastrous for Indians, occurring as it did during the celebration of the hun-dredth birthday of the United States. An angry and patriotically charged America demanded that the federal government avenge Custer's death and solve once and for all the Indian "problem."

Volunteers across the nation offered to march into the West to destroy Indians. Newspapers demanded retribution. "Killing a mess of Indian is the only recreation our frontier rangers want," the *Dallas Daily Herald* cried out.[97]

A few white leaders, though, condemned Custer's actions. "I regard Custer's massacre as a sacrifice of troops, brought on by Custer himself, that was wholly unnecessary," President Ulysses S. Grant told the *New York Herald*. "He was not to have made the attack before [the arrival of reinforcements]."[98]

Nonetheless, the government mobilized its troops to punish the Plains Indians. Within months, blue-coated soldiers hunted down and defeated the northern Cheyenne in Montana's Powder River country and the Sioux in South Dakota along Cedar Creek.

Then in the spring of 1877, three thousand more Cheyenne and Sioux, including Crazy Horse, the greatest warrior of the northern plains, surrendered in the face of endless, relentless pounding by American artillery.

The once defiant Indians who had roamed the Great Plains free and independent now faced a bleak and heartbreaking removal to reservations in Indian Territory near the Missouri River. Indian power on the northern plains seemed as dead as Yellow Hair himself.

I Will Fight No More Forever

Though the Sioux War marked the last major Indian war, one final act of Indian resistance remained to be carried out by the Nez Percé (pierced nose) tribe.

During the 1850s, whites first appeared on Nez Percé lands in Idaho and Oregon. Yielding to the inevitable demands for their land, the Nez Percé ceded a section of their territory and relocated to government reservations. However, this concession did little to appease white desire; in 1877 the government compelled the Nez Percé to move again, this time to the Lapwai Reservation in Idaho.

While the move was under way, a group of white settlers tried to steal horses from the Nez Percé, provoking warriors to launch a series of deadly retaliatory raids.

Fearing military reprisals, Chief Joseph of the Nez Percé led his people—150 warriors and 550 other men, women, and children and their famous spotted horses—on a wild and daring seventeen-hundred-mile escape through Montana and Wyoming toward safe haven in Canada.

Wearied, tattered, and hungry, the Nez Percé faltered just forty miles shy of the Canadian border, where the army intercepted

Crazy Horse and his people begin their solemn journey to surrender to the U.S. government.

"I Will Fight No More Forever"

This passage, taken from Native American Testimony, *edited by Peter Nabokov, reproduces Chief Joseph's poignant words of surrender on October 4, 1887, to Col. Nelson Miles and Gen. O. O. Howard.*

"Tell General Howard I know his heart. What he told me before, I have in my heart.

I am tired of fighting. Our chiefs are killed. Looking Glass [a Nez Percé chief] is dead. Toohoolhoolzote [a prophet] is dead. The old men are all dead.

It is the young men who say yes and no. He who led on the young men is dead. It is cold and we have no blankets. The little children are freezing to death.

My people, some of them, have run away to the hills, and have no blankets, no food; no one knows where they are—perhaps freezing to death.

I want to have time to look for my children and see how many I can find. Maybe I shall find them among the dead.

From where the sun now stands I will fight no more forever."

them. After a five-day battle, the Indians, starving and wounded, reluctantly agreed to the terms offered by Col. Nelson Miles: "If you will come out and give up your arms, I will spare your lives and send you to your reservation."[99]

Although a few Nez Percé warriors managed to escape, most of the tribe surrendered, expecting to be returned to Idaho as Miles had promised. But they were grievously mistaken. Ignoring Miles's objections, the army ordered the Nez Percé to live in Indian Territory. Here Joseph's six children and a full one-fourth of his tribe died from disease and grief.

In 1885, believing that Chief Joseph and 150 others might again stir up the Nez Percé, the government shipped the Indians to the Coville Reservation in Washington to remain isolated from their loved ones for the rest of their lives. Here, on September 1, 1904, the reservation's doctor wrote that Chief Joseph had died of a "broken heart."

The Final Mopping Up

After the surrender of the Nez Percé, it was but a matter of time until all isolated pockets of Indian resistance were mopped up completely. On Indian Territory, soldiers crushed Kiowa and Comanche rebellions led by Quannah Parker on the southern plains. In 1878 an uprising by Utes of Colorado was stamped out. The same fate awaited the Klamath in southern Oregon. In 1881 Sitting Bull and his band of Sioux surrendered at Fort Buford, North Dakota. In the Southwest in 1886, after years of marauding and raiding the whites in New Mexico and Arizona, the fabled warrior chief Geronimo and his band of Apaches became prisoners of the Americans.

By now the West had visibly changed. Railroads and telegraph wires stretched over the vastness, cutting across the trails of the near-extinct buffalo and former Indian lands. Towns sprang up along railroad tracks. Mine shafts were dug. Barbed wire fences marked off the boundaries of the settlers. And everywhere in the great West, Indian tribes were smashed and decimated, their members corralled onto cramped, barren reservations.

The Ghost Dance and Wounded Knee

Arising from the gloom, despair, disease, and poverty of the shattered and displaced Indians came a great vision—the Dreamer Religion. Begun by the prophet Smoholla, a Wanapum Indian in the Northwest, the Dreamer Religion was a mixture of Indian and Christian beliefs that called on Indians to reject white culture and dominance. Only by doing this, insisted Smoholla, could Indians get back their lost lands.

An important part of this spiritual movement was the Ghost Dance, a ritual introduced by another prophet, a Paiute named Wovoka, who said that during a solar eclipse

Chief Joseph surrenders amid the corpses of his fallen people. Joseph attempted to flee with members of his tribe, mostly women and children, into Canada.

he had received a vision from the Great Spirit with a message for Indians. Author Annette Rosenstiel, in *Red & White: Indian Views of the White Man 1492–1982,* explains:

> They were to give up European—now American—ways, return to the old customs practiced before the Europeans arrived, and to the simple life, with no guns, no alcohol, and no trade goods. And, if the Indians performed the Ghost Dance, the religion's chief ritual, the whites would disappear, the land would be returned to the Indian people, and all the great warriors of former times would come back to earth.[100]

The Ghost Dance lasted for days at a time as Indians danced to the hypnotic pounding of drums. Some warriors wore "ghost shirts," which they believed would make them immune to the white man's bullets. On the reservations, men, women, and children danced and danced, waiting for a Christ-like savior to come.

As one tribe after another adopted the haunting Ghost Dance, with its feverish vision of a final struggle with the whites, a reunion with dead ancestors, and a restoration of the nearly vanished buffalo herds, nearby settlers and miners began to worry about an Indian uprising in the foreseeable future. Government Indian agents also fretted.

In mid-November 1890, a terrified employee at the Sioux reservation in Pine Ridge, South Dakota, telegraphed, "Indians are dancing in the snow and are wild and crazy. . . . We need protection and we need it now. The leaders should be arrested and confined at some military post until the matter is quieted, and this should be done at once."[101]

Local authorities summoned Custer's old regiment, the Seventh Cavalry, to be on hand in case of violence. They also forbid the Ghost Dance from continuing and ordered the arrest of Indians suspected of stirring up a rebellion. But when the great leader Sitting Bull was killed resisting arrest on a reservation, grief-stricken Sioux

One of the staunchest opponents to U.S. takeover was Geronimo, here shown with his family after having been taken prisoner at Fort Sill.

Arapaho participate in the Ghost Dance in an attempt to revitalize Indian power.

mourners danced themselves into an even greater frenzy.

In December 1890, during a climate of rising tension on the reservations, a Sioux chief named Big Foot was leading a band of men, women, and children to join the main tribe of Sioux dancing in the Badlands when the group were confronted by troops of the Seventh Cavalry. The soldiers carried orders to arrest Big Foot, one of the suspected "fomenters of disturbances."[102]

Big Foot's people did not resist. They peacefully traveled with the soldiers toward a nearby fort. On December 28, 1890, the Indians, under guard, camped along a creek called Wounded Knee. The next morning, army troops grew uneasy. Circling the Indi-

ans with huge Hotchkiss guns, they ordered the Sioux to surrender their weapons.

Bearing in mind massacres of other Indians in the past, the Sioux grew fearful and suspicious and refused. Suddenly a shot was fired—no one knows by whom—and instantly the U.S. Army raked the Indians with blazing gunfire, killing ninety men and two hundred women and children. "We tried to run," recalled Louise Weasel Bear, "but they shot us like we were buffalo."[103]

Many bled to death in the snow. The soldiers stacked the frozen corpses into a mass grave and posed for photographs. Later, Congress awarded twenty-six Medals of Honor to troops who had carried out the slaughter.

At last, armed Indian resistance was finished. After four centuries of relentless effort, whites had conquered an entire continent and subdued its native people.

The Aftermath of War

While many Americans considered the American conquest with sorrow, others expressed no regret. This attitude was represented by future president Theodore Roosevelt who wrote in *Winning of the West* in 1889:

Looking back, it is easy to say that much of the wrong-doing could have been prevented, but if we examine the facts . . . we are bound to admit that the struggle was really one that could not possibly have been avoided. . . . Unless we were willing that the whole continent west of the Alleghenies should remain an unpeopled waste, the hunting-ground of savages, war was inevitable; and even had we been willing, and had we refrained from encroaching on the Indians' lands, the war would have come nevertheless, for

After U.S. troops massacred Indians at Wounded Knee, they stacked frozen corpses into a mass grave.

The frozen corpse of Sioux chief Big Foot lies in the snow after the Battle of Wounded Knee. Big Foot tried to cooperate with whites in an attempt to protect the lives of women and children.

then the Indians themselves would have encroached on ours.[104]

Native Americans, of course, were hardly philosophical; they were angry, depressed, and grief stricken. Buffalo Bird Woman, of the Hidatsa tribe, recorded her sadness:

Sometimes at evening I sit, looking out on the big Missouri [River]. The sun sets, and dusk steals over the water. In the shadows I seem again to see our Indian village, with smoke curling upward from the earth lodges; and in the river's road I hear the yells of the warriors, the laughter of little children as of old. It is but an old woman's dream. Again I see but shadows and hear only the roar of the river; and tears come into my eyes. Our Indian life, I know is gone forever.[105]

Thus, at long last, the question, "Whose land is it?" had been resolved on many battlefields. The debate was finished.

But burning new questions emerged: What about the 200,000 Indians who were left alive? Where should they dwell? How should they live? Who was responsible for these deposed and disinherited people?

8 Trying to Make Indians White

During the second half of the nineteenth century, nearly all Native Americans lived on a hundred Indian reservations—most of them in the West—set up by the federal government. In 1871, in fact, Gen. Philip Sheridan, the commander of the military operation on the Great Plains, forbade Indians to leave their reservations without the proper pass from white authorities.

Indians living on a reservation are issued supplies by members of the U.S. government. Deprived of a way to make a living, Indians became totally dependent on whites.

One of Geronimo's warriors called the confined Indians "prisoners of war."

During this time, a branch of the Department of the Interior, the Bureau of Indian Affairs (BIA), emerged as the federal organization most responsible for dealing with the Indians. Though often corrupt and inept, the BIA provided food, clothing, and basic moral and educational instruction to Indians. But the agency did not treat humanely the people it was supposed to serve. Reservation Indians, in fact, were routinely harassed by whites for their alleged savage, pagan, or lazy ways. "There is no question of national dignity . . . involved in the treatment of savages by a civilized power," Indian commissioner Francis Walker instructed whites who had dealings with Indians. "With wild men as with beasts, the question whether in any given situation one shall fight, coax, or run, is a question of which is safest."[106]

For the federal government, the reservation system made logistical sense. As a superintendent of the BIA once remarked, "In history the U.S. government discovered that it was cheaper to keep [the Indians] on the reservations than to try and kill them. So, they were marched into what we hoped were useless pieces of land."[107]

But to Native Americans, the federal reservations meant disaster. Defeated in

A Call for Justice

These introductory remarks from Helen Hunt Jackson's book A Century of Dishonor, *published in 1881, were meant to arouse public debate over the treatment of American Indians.*

"The history of the United States Government's repeated violations of faith with the Indian thus convicts us, as a nation, not only of having outraged the principles of justice, which are the basis of international law . . . but of having made ourselves liable to all punishments, which follow upon such sins. . . .

There is but one hope of righting this wrong. It lies in appeal to the heart and the conscience of the American people. What the people demanded, Congress will do . . . .

What an opportunity for the Congress of 1880 to cover itself with a lustre of glory, as the first to cut short our nation's record of cruelties and perjuries! The first attempt to redeem the name of the United States from the stain of a century of dishonor!"

war, uprooted from their tribal lands, they were now completely at the mercy of whites for their protection and welfare. "I think you had better put the Indians on wheels," Red Dog, a Sioux chief, bitterly complained to white treaty makers in 1876. "Then you can run them about whenever you wish."[108]

No longer could Native Americans negotiate treaties with the federal government. They lost this right in 1871, when Congress voted to stop treating Indians as separate nations as had been done, at least in theory, since colonial times. Although Congress claimed it would honor treaties made before 1871, it declined to negotiate any new ones. But this promise was hardly reassuring to most Indians, since the federal government had violated almost all the four hundred treaties it had made. From this moment onward, Indians were

to be considered wards—as if they were children. Instead of having the power to negotiate treaties, they would be subject to congressional laws and agreements, and presidential decrees.

This drastic policy change proved disastrous for Native Americans. Stripped of their status as sovereign peoples, they faced a long future of legal challenges by non-Indians.

Worse still, Congress, freed from the constraints of treaties, periodically cut off or reduced its "annuities" to Indians. And even supplies that had been funded often failed to arrive in Indian hands because many unscrupulous Indian agents diverted them to the black market for their own profit. This meant that Native Americans faced increased incidence of malnutrition, disease, and mental illness.

Indian Reform or Ruin?

Many Americans, including some white BIA employees and army officers, were appalled by the government's poor treatment of Native Americans and worked for reform of federal Indian policy. Their efforts received a boost in 1881 when writer and Indian sympathizer Helen Hunt Jackson published *A Century of Dishonor,* a powerful work that raised public awareness of the dismal history of forced Indian removal. Both this work and Jackson's novel *Ramona* stirred the American conscience much as Harriet Beecher Stowe's *Uncle Tom's Cabin* had caused Americans to question the institution of slavery in the decade or so before the Civil War.

As the twentieth century approached, powerful political groups in Washington reached a consensus: Reformers and Indian haters alike agreed that it was no longer possible for Indians to live traditional nomadic lives; instead, they argued that Indians had to be assimilated into America's mainstream life and culture. And the best way to do this, insisted the politicians, was to strip Indians of their traditional ways and convert them from wandering hunters into sedentary farmers. Furthermore, many reformers wanted Native Americans to become English-speaking Christians who would take part in the American capitalistic economic system.

During the 1880s, well-meaning, but perhaps culturally misguided white preachers, teachers, and various volunteers descended on the reservations to attempt to replace Indian languages, customs, and religions with their own ways. The federal government joined the effort. This official move brought praise in an 1888 report from the Board of Indian Commissioners:

> The day when it [the policy to reduce tribal authority] was approved by the president [Grover Cleveland] may be called the Indians' emancipation day. It gives the Indian the possibility to become a man instead of remaining a

Chiricahua Apaches upon arrival at Carlisle Indian School (left), and after being appropriately dressed to enter the white world (right). Such schools took young members of various tribes and molded them to fit into white society.

ward of the government. It affords to him the opportunity to make for himself and his family a home, and to live among his equals a manly and independent life.[109]

Believing education to be the best way to facilitate assimilation for Indians, the government set up hundreds of day schools and many boarding schools, such as Pennsylvania's Carlisle Indian School, to teach young Indians the basics of living like whites in such areas as cooking, mechanics, and farming. Often Indian children were uprooted from their tribes and sent far away to live and learn at the white schools. Sometimes they were punished by preachers or former military officers at the schools for trying to escape or for clinging to familiar ways. Some school authorities punished Indian children for speaking their own languages. In addition, reports Indian historian Little Rock Reed:

> By the mid-1800s, the United States had banned most forms of Indian religion on the reservations. Indians who maintained tribal customs were subject to imprisonment, forced labor, and even punishment by starvation. Indian dress, ceremony, dances, and singing were forbidden. Sacred instruments, medicine, and pipes were confiscated and destroyed. Even Indian names and hairstyles were forbidden by law.[110]

The net results of such governmental actions was to weaken Indian family unity, undermine tribal authority, degrade Indian culture, and help pitch Indians into depths of despair.

Making matters worse for Native Americans was a conviction among many whites across the nation, even some who were sympathetic to Indians, that the apparent demise of Indian peoples was "scientifically" determined, and therefore justifiable.

Claims of White Superiority

For centuries, Europeans who did not distinguish between the spirituality of native North American people and the religiousness found among many whites had generally looked down on Indians. But the idea of white superiority assumed a new form of racist thinking that developed, in part, from the work of English naturalist Charles Darwin in the mid-nineteenth century. In essence, Darwin argued that all life on earth had changed through the ages from simple life forms to more complex ones. Ruthless competition for food and water among living creatures, he claimed, resulted in the "survival of the fittest" and the disappearance, or extinction, of the weakest.

Although Darwin never used his ideas to explain human behavior, other writers did. By the 1890s, in fact, some authors were arguing that whites were the "fittest" race in the world, and Indians, among others, had become a "vanishing race." This type of reasoning, called social Darwinism, gave encouragement to unsympathetic whites who had the power to determine the survival of Indians.

In 1898, for example, Sen. Albert Beveridge of Indiana argued that "God . . . has made [English-speaking white people] that master organizers of the world. . . . He has made us adept in government [so] that we may administer government among savages and servile people."[111]

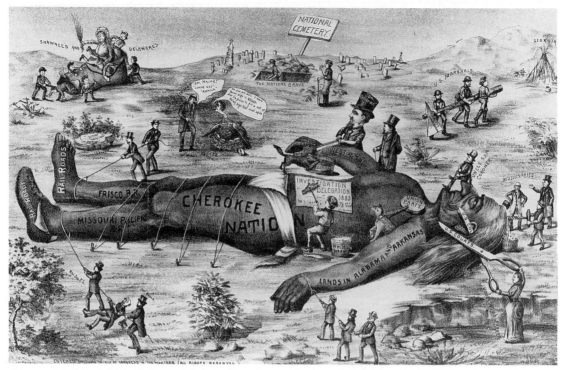

A cartoon satirizes white treatment of Indians. In a scene reminiscent of Gulliver's
Travels, *Lilliputian whites subdue a giant Indian who symbolizes a lost civilization.*

Francis Leupp, a commissioner of Indian Affairs, also gave a Darwinian twist to an argument sometimes advanced with respect to Indian land rights. Indians and other "uncivilized peoples," he said, wasted natural resources, and it was just a matter of time until the "civilized" world encroached on and overpowered them. "Hence the most we can ask of the advanced race," Leupp wrote, "is to deal justly with the backward races and give always a fair equivalent for the land it invades."[112]

The Dawes Act

In 1887 Congress responded to growing public pressure to act more effectively on the "Indian problem." To the applause of reformers, it passed the Dawes Severalty—or General Allotment—Act, named for its sponsor, Sen. Henry L. Dawes of Massachusetts. At last, it seemed to many whites, the country was creating a humane and wise program to help the displaced Indians.

The purpose of the Dawes Act was to transform Indians into independent farmers. To achieve this goal, federal agents surveyed Indian land, evicted trespassers, and then reapportioned or "allotted" smaller sections of land back to the Indians on a severalty or *individual* basis, rather than a tribal one. Each family, for example, received 160 acres, while unmarried adults and orphans under the age of eighteen obtained half that amount. Forty acres went to children who lived with their parents. Twice as much land could be allotted if the property in question was suitable for grazing but not for farming.

The act also provided a boon to whites. Federal agents designated as "surplus" any lands left over after all allotments had been made. Such lands could be sold to non-Indians. The proceeds of these sales were earmarked to buy supplies for Indians.

At first, the Dawes Act also stipulated that "allotted Indians" could receive U.S. citizenship. But with this provision came a problem: as citizens, Indians would have to pay property taxes; but if they were unable to meet their assessments, they would be liable to lose their lands to whites.

Once made aware of this shortcoming, Congress responded by amending the act. The revised version allowed the government to hold all allotted Indian lands in trust for twenty-five years. During this period, Indians were exempt from paying taxes. But Congress also prohibited the sale of allotted lands, hoping to protect the Indians from squandering their holdings or being fleeced by underhanded land agents. When the trust period was over, the government was obliged to issue formal deeds that allowed Indian landowners to do with their land as they pleased.

At first, liberal reformers and humanitarians had high hopes for the Dawes Act. They believed the program would help Indians to assimilate successfully into American life. Many conservatives also favored the act, but for an entirely different reason. They believed that the initial reservation system had unwisely set aside too much public land to Indians—a people who were a "vanishing race." But with an allotment system in place, they reasoned, Indian lands held by individuals, rather than tribes, could more easily be transferred away from their rightful owners.

Failure of Allotment

"By allotting reservation land in severalty," writes Janet A. McDonnell in *The Dispossession of the American Indian, 1887–1934*, "policy makers hoped to replace tribal civilization with a white one, protect the Indians from unscrupulous whites, promote progress and save the federal government money."[113]

Despite the good intentions of its supporters, though, the Dawes Act was catastrophic for Indians. During the forty-seven years of its existence, Indians experienced enormous land losses—the very thing reformers had wished to avoid. The reasons for this colossal failure lay in the provisions of the act itself.

From the onset, tribal authority suffered a blow when the government parceled out land to individuals instead of to the tribes as communities. This break with tradition came on the heels of another setback, the Major Crimes Act of 1885, which allowed the federal government, instead of tribal authorities, to mete out punishments for felonies committed on the reservations. While many whites may have been pleased with any outcome that reduced Indian power, Native Americans were generally distraught to realize that yet another element of their way of life was vanishing.

The provisions of the Dawes Act were supposed to turn Indians into self-sufficient farmers who would learn to "stand on their own feet" and wean themselves from government assistance. But this goal was very hard to accomplish. For one thing, some Indians had become dependent on government rations and saw no need to farm. Many Indian males despised the idea of farming. They believed that agriculture was "women's work" unsuitable for hunters and warriors. Some opposed farming for reasons involving the relationship of the individual to the earth.

Even the Indians who did take up farming encountered many problems that often doomed their best efforts. Much of the land allotted to Native Americans was barren, naturally arid and without access to water. Not only did Indians generally lack experience in modern farming techniques, they seldom had sufficient equipment, seed, and livestock to get started in agriculture. Often the federal government failed to provide loans adequate to permit Indians to buy these necessary items.

Inheritance problems also marred Indian attempts at farming. If an Indian died before his trust period had ended, his heirs divided his property. As these lands were passed down from one generation to the next, however, they were divided into smaller and smaller units until finally they were too small to farm economically. Then, unable to use these diminished parcels, Indians once again sold their land to white speculators.

In some cases, Indians complained that federal agents deliberately allotted the most desirable lands to Native Americans who were not full-blooded Indians, who resold the land to nonwhites with suspicious rapidity.

Often white officials carried out allotment hastily and thoughtlessly, without giving much consideration to whether lands were suitable for anyone to use.

At one of the many trade schools set up to assimilate Indians, young men learn to be blacksmiths.

After being subdued, dominated, and forced onto Indian Territory (Oklahoma), Indians lose the final battle as whites decide to settle the territory, leaving no area remaining for the North American Indian.

"Even on reservations so crowded with trees one could not walk the lands or in barren desert areas, allotment was carried out in defiance of common sense because Congress had so decreed," writes Indian activist and author Vine Deloria.[114]

Eventually Congress took action to prevent further damage to Indian holdings by allowing Native Americans to sell property that had been inherited before the expiration of the trust period and to split the profits among the heirs. Although this new rule was meant to help Indians, it actually quickened the pace of sales of Indian lands to eager white buyers.

Many Native Americans—especially the very young and the very old—were simply incapable of farming. They had little use for their allotments. Thus, in 1891 Congress amended the Dawes Act to allow Indians "by reason of age or other disability" to lease their lands to non-Indians, if the U.S. Department of the Interior approved.

Three years later, "inability to farm" was added by federal lawmakers as another reason Indians could cite in seeking permission to lease their lands. Once again, the change merely made it easier for land-hungry whites to obtain Indian lands.

But allotment was not the only means used in the late nineteenth century to pry land away from Native Americans. Other forces were also at work, particularly in Oklahoma.

The Oklahoma Land Seizure

By the late 1880s, what was left of Indian Territory was under siege. For years, federal troops tried without much success to keep land-hungry settlers out of Oklahoma. Finally Congress gave in to pressure and opened to homesteading two million acres of the "Unassigned Lands" or Oklahoma District in the western part of the territory. On April 22, 1889, sixty thousand people rushed into Oklahoma to stake their claims. Other such "land runs" took place over the next six years, as the former Indian Territory was sliced smaller, strip by strip, until all that was left were lands directly held by the Five Civilized Tribes.

But these lands too were soon carved up in allotment by the Dawes Act. Surplus land, once again, landed in white possession.

Indian Territory Incorporated into the United States

For decades, one of the greatest fears expressed by Indians in negotiations with whites was the prospect of seeing their lands incorporated into a state or federal territory. Repeatedly government officials assured Indian leaders that such a thing would never take place.

But in 1897, yet another official white promise vaporized when President William McKinley announced that Indian Territory was to become part of the United States.

Ten years later, Oklahoma and the fragmentary remains of the Indian Territory became the forty-sixth state of the United States. As Indians and federal agents squabbled over the details of allotment, many impatient, unscrupulous whites contrived ways to take possession of Indian lands. Often they squatted illegally on Indian Territory, tricked Indians out of their properties, and even killed to get what they wanted. Unaware of the true value of their allotted parcels and confused by the concept of landownership, many Indians sold their lands much too cheaply.

Land Acquisition by Stealth

Stealth was a common method of obtaining ownership of Indian lands. For instance, the original treaty that set up the Kiowa and Comanche reservations clearly required that any sale of Indian reservation land be approved by three-fourths of a tribe's adult males. Such legal protection notwithstanding, federal agents quietly worked out an agreement with only a few Indian representatives, who agreed to sell tribal lands to whites. In 1903 an Indian named Lone Wolf challenged this treaty violation in a lawsuit that ultimately was heard by the U.S. Supreme Court.

Lone Wolf challenged a treaty that allowed whites to buy land from Indians, but lost. His fight resulted in even fewer rights for Indians.

Lone Wolf lost. Worse still, his legal effort only made conditions worse for American Indians. In its decision, the Court deemed that the federal government was free to treat its wards as it saw fit, including ignoring treaty obligations if this proved convenient.

Thus, Indians now had no legal way of preventing the federal government from breaking up reservations or doing anything else it wanted against Indians. But the government had always done as it pleased.

The Landgrab Continues

Even after Oklahoma acquired statehood and millions of acres of Indian land became available for whites to buy or take, the pressure to seize Indian land continued. Again, whites alleged that Indians were not suitable caretakers for the parcels of land that remained in their hands.

"I hold it to be an economic and social crime in this age and under modern conditions," insisted Cato Sells, commissioner of Indian Affairs in 1913, "to permit thousands of acres of fertile land belonging to the Indians and capable of great industrial development to lie in unproductive idleness."[115]

Two years later, the BIA enabled whites to obtain such lands more easily by changing the Dawes Act to allow "competent" Indians to be exempt from the

An advertisement offers Indian lands for sale. Once masters of an entire continent, Indians' last remaining parcels were opened to white settlement.

twenty-five-year trust period. This change meant that landowners aged twenty-one, with at least a sixth grade education and at least one Indian parent could dispose of their lands as they pleased. The end result of the BIA's action was an even greater selloff of lands to whites.

Meanwhile, a catastrophic event was unfolding in Europe that would soon indirectly cause even greater loss of Indian lands: the First World War.

9 Forced into the Twentieth Century

The entry of the United States into the First World War in 1917 created a huge demand for food for the military forces of the nation and its European allies. And to help meet this necessity, the federal government pressured Indians to use more of their lands for agriculture or to lease them to people who would grow crops. To speed up the process, the government removed restrictions on many Indian land sales.

Across the West, many Indians responded as the government had requested. When the war ended in 1918, however, European nations resumed producing most of their own food. Thus the demand for U.S. farm products sank, causing a stunning fall in both food and land lease prices. At the same time, nature dealt the Indians and other farmers an extra blow. Terrible droughts and a severe winter in the West compounded their economic problems. To pay off staggering debts, many Indians went bankrupt and had no choice but to sell their lands to the ever-waiting whites.

Fueling the appetite for Indian land at this time was an increasing movement by whites to the western lands. Historian Janet McDonnell describes this demographic shift:

> From 1890 to 1920, the population of the country jumped from 63,000,000 to 106,000,000, a 68-percent increase, prompting settlers to push into the arid

After thousands of whites moved west in the nineteenth century, the population boomed, increasing the demand for remaining Indian lands.

John Collier became commissioner of Indian Affairs in 1934. Collier wrote legislation that attempted to halt the seizure of Indian lands.

and semi-arid regions of the West. As the cost of farmland soared, the "free" land of the public domain and the surplus land on Indian reservations became more appealing. Whites who saw the supply of valuable land shrinking now demanded that Indian land be developed and managed efficiently. It was no longer enough for Indians to accept allotments and surrender the surplus land to whites; they were expected to use their own allotted land profitably or surrender it.[116]

And so during the 1920s and 1930s, Indians continued to sell, lease, and lose their lands to whites at an alarming rate. By 1934 the outlook for American Indians was grim. Since 1887 Indian land holdings had shrunk from 138 million acres to 52 million acres. Two-thirds of all Indians either were landless or lacked enough land to make a living. These Native Americans became even more dependent on the gov-ernment, creating a situation exactly the opposite of what reformers had in mind when the Dawes Act was launched.

A New Deal for American Indians?

But in 1933 the United States had a new chief executive, Franklin Delano Roosevelt, whose views differed radically from those of all the other U.S. presidents who had held office since the Dawes Act was passed in 1887. Indians believed that at last they had a defender in high office.

In 1934 Roosevelt appointed John Collier, a champion of the Indian cause, to the position of commissioner of Indian Affairs. A longtime champion and student of Indian culture, Collier was a former teacher and social worker who wanted the government to drastically overhaul its Indian policy to help Native Americans.

One of Collier's major accomplishments was to help write the Indian Reorganization Act of 1934. This piece of legislation halted allotment and banned unregulated sales of Indian lands. Furthermore, it authorized the government to buy back "surplus" lands whenever possible and restore them to tribal hands. After the act's passage, the government spent $70 million in three years building new schools, clinics, roads, community centers, irrigation systems, and other community projects on Indian reservations.

The act also was meant to strengthen tribal authority by empowering American Indians to govern themselves with elected representatives. Tribal corporations were to be formed to work toward economic development for the tribes.

Indian participation in World War II left many Native Americans with a renewed sense of pride and determination to resist the second-class treatment awarded them by whites.

Collier did even more on behalf of Indians. One of his first acts was to lift the ban against Indian religious ceremonies on reservations, which had been in effect for several decades. He also hired more Native Americans to work in his agency and set up instruction classes on Indian languages and culture on reservations.

Unsurprisingly, however, Collier amassed a slew of critics—many of them conservative white lawmakers in Congress—who thought he had gone too far in using government resources to assist Indians. In the early 1940s, these critics received an unexpected boost in their campaign against Collier's ideas from another global catastrophe: the Second World War.

Second World War: A Turning Point

The Second World War dramatically changed the lives of Indians, as well as many other Americans who had been ex-

cluded from the mainstream of American life. Some twenty-five thousand Indian men fought in the war and distinguished themselves as fighters, radio operators, and code breakers. Personally changed by their foreign travels and wartime experiences, many returned home when the war ended in 1945, self-confident and determined to resist the low-class status imposed on them by whites.

Other Native Americans left the reservations during the war to work in defense plants and other factories, doing jobs formerly performed almost exclusively by white men. As a result, Indians proved to themselves and others that they could function successfully in the white world. Also, thanks to the passage of the Snyder Act in 1924, American Indians had both U.S. citizenship and the right to vote, which increased their political strength.

When the war ended, John Collier and his Indian policies became vulnerable to the attacks of conservative opponents, who sensed that the political climate had changed in their favor. Now some even accused Collier of fostering "un-American" ideas such as trying to keep Native Americans separate from mainstream America. Collier resigned in 1945 in a whirlwind of controversy.

Next, many congressional critics attacked all Indian programs, arguing that it was time to get out of the "Indian business." They cited an influential report from a panel of experts called the Hoover Commission on Governmental Efficiency, which had concluded that through their war experience, Native Americans had demonstrated they were quite capable of surviving in the modern world without government help. Government payments of support to Indians, which had begun as annuities in the nineteenth century, were now, according to some, too expensive and unnecessary. In 1946, for example, Congressman O. K. Chandler of Oklahoma complained to a fellow lawmaker that the country could expect to have spent up to $2 billion on Indians by 1996. "They do not need a Federal

A Seneca woman enlists in the Navy in this 1943 picture. Many Native Americans left the reservation during the war, never to return.

guardian now," he argued, "nor will they need one for the next 50 years!"[117]

Another Oklahoma congressman, George Schwabe, went even further and called for the abolition of the BIA. "It is a drain upon the taxpayers," he insisted, "[and] a poor guardian for the Indians. I think it tends to encourage paternalism and socialist and . . . communistic thinking."[118]

Many Americans agreed with Schwabe's criticism of the BIA. They also shared his concern over communism. At the time, the Soviet Union with its communist form of government seemed to offer a serious threat to American security. Moreover, a strong feeling of wartime unity and supercharged patriotism still existed in America. All these factors combined resulted in strong pressure on all U.S. citizens—including Indians—to conform to conservative views.

Thus during the late 1940s many Republicans in Congress demanded a new federal Indian policy—one based on termination. This approach, formulated by the Hoover Commission, included plans to dismantle Indian reservations, undo all treaties, cancel all federal responsibilities for Indian welfare, and end Indian tribal life forever. By these acts, advocates of termination hoped to reverse Collier's efforts to promote self-determination for Indian tribes. They preferred instead to attempt to assimilate Indians into mainstream American life.

The Termination Idea

But the termination idea was controversial. Whites argued among themselves over it. So did Native Americans. And often the split among Indians was racially determined. Historian Donald Lee Fixico stated these positions in *Termination and Relocation: Federal Indian Policy in the 1950s*:

> The Indian view was divided. Those who agreed with federal officials were primarily mixed-bloods, while those who believed that Indians were still considerably different from white Americans were full-bloods.
>
> Many mixed-bloods stated that they were tired of government restrictions on their properties and wanted them lifted. They professed that the federal trust status made Indians second-class citizens. The majority of this group of Indians was ready to join the mainstream society, but the full-blood faction objected.[119]

Full-bloods, in fact, were generally appalled by the idea of termination. They greatly feared that it would bring cultural annihilation, the end of their values and traditions. And they suspected that once again, white lawmakers were conniving to turn Indian lands over to white timber, ranching, mineral, and real estate interests.

As the termination movement gained strength, another idea concerning Indians also became popular with lawmakers: letting Indians have a chance to seek monetary rewards for the losses they had sustained at the hands of the federal government.

The Indian Claims Commission

In 1946 Congress passed legislation allowing Indians to bring lawsuits against the United States before a body called the Indian Claims Commission. Liberal supporters of this idea maintained that at long last Indians had a chance to receive at least cash payments for their great land losses.

Some lawmakers, however, angrily denounced the plan. "Why must we buy America from the Indian all over again?" demanded one Republican congressman in 1946.[120]

During the next decade, Indians collected more than $500 million in settle-

Seminole vote after being awarded the privilege by the Snyder Act, passed in 1924.

President Truman at the signing of the Indian Claims Commission bill that allowed Indians to bring lawsuits against the government to regain or be paid for land taken unlawfully by the U.S. government.

ments for loss of lands taken during the nineteenth century. Over a thirty-year period, they won 101 cases and lost 133.

But during the late 1940s, the pro-termination lawmakers pounced on the claims policy, arguing that the lawsuits were enriching Indians so greatly that all other means of federal economic assistance should be ended. Many conservatives now argued that once the claims process had run its course, Congress would be able to say it had met its final financial obligation to Native Americans. Then, the government could disclaim any future responsibility for Indians. To do so, however, could lead to further disaster for Native Americans. By 1950, for example, more than half of all Indians lived on reservations, the rest in cities. No matter where they resided, however, they were America's poorest ethnic group.

Despite the allure of much-needed money, some Indian tribes refused cash settlements even without the option to reclaim their lands. Said a chief of the Blackfoot tribe to white government officials:

Our land is more valuable than your money. It will last forever. It will not even perish by the flames of fire. . . . We cannot sell the lives of men and animals; therefore we cannot sell this land. It was put here by the Great Spirit and we cannot sell it because it does not belong to us![121]

An Era of Termination

In 1953 President Dwight D. Eisenhower, a conservative Republican who had had a distinguished military career as a leader in the Second World War and, later, of the North American Treaty Organization (NATO), officially implemented a termination policy.

House Concurrent Resolution 108, the piece of legislation that legalized the termination plan, stated: "Indian tribes . . . and individual members . . . should be freed from Federal Supervision and control."[122]

This language meant that the government could end its protection of and responsibilities for all Indian groups. The government could dissolve reservations that were homes for thousands of Indians and disperse the tribes' assets.

Congress also directed the BIA to commence a relocation program for Indians, moving them from reservations to urban areas, where they were expected to become self-sufficient city dwellers. To hasten the process, the government imposed a new rule on Indians: All tribes had to agree to submit to the termination policy *before* they could press further claims against the government for past land losses.

From 1954 to 1962, there were 109 tribes, bands, and other Indian groups officially liquidated by federal termination policy. These actions, argued supporters of the policy, helped Indians by eliminating the racial stigma of tribal status.

In reality, though, most Indians suffered terribly. Many saw their reservations and tribal identities vanish. Alone in the concrete canyons of American big cities, they experienced cultural shock and racial discrimination. Many Indians were unskilled and unemployable workers who found themselves reduced to abject poverty. Their health and life expectancies were the lowest in the nation; their suicide rate was double that of the general population.

Often termination plunged tribal communities into economic disaster. One of the saddest examples of such a fall took place in 1958 on the Menominee reservation in Wisconsin. After the government broke up the reservation into privately owned land tracts, the Menominee were forced to raise money for land taxes, something most Indians could not afford. Thus, they decided to pool their assets by placing all their properties and a tribe-owned sawmill under the control of a Menominee corporation.

This decision proved disastrous when financial hard times came and tribal leaders were forced to sell to whites a controlling interest in the enterprise, plus Indian hunting and fishing lands. Within a few years, the corporation verged on bankruptcy; as a result, the Menominee people suffered from severe poverty, unemployment, and health problems.

In 1958 the Eisenhower administration realized that termination was a huge mistake and stopped implementing the policy unless Indians requested it. (In 1975 the government restored to the Menominee their tribal status and reservation.) According to Vine Deloria:

The termination policy simply evaporated in the early 1960s because not enough advocates could be found in Congress to make it an important issue. By 1958, Indians were beginning to go to the polls in increasingly larger numbers and would retaliate against senators and congressmen who suggested a break in the traditional federal–Indian relationship. Many persons in Congress might have wanted to sever the relationship, but it was a hazardous position to maintain at election time.[123]

Rising Militancy

In 1961 a huge group of Indians gathered at the University of Chicago to initiate a bold first step in self-assertion by issuing a Declaration of Indian Purpose. Put together by 420 Indians from 67 tribes, this document launched a modern Indian rights movement. Among other things, it called on the federal government to restore lost reservations, improve the quality of life for Indians, and begin a major effort to reform the BIA into an agency more responsive to Indian problems.

When satisfactory changes were not forthcoming, many young Indians grew increasingly militant. Following the examples of black activists and other protesters of the turbulent 1960s, they resorted to radical solutions to dramatize their frustrations.

For instance, in 1968, members of the National Indian Youth Council (NIYC) staged flagrantly illegal "fish-ins" in Washington State to protest government restrictions on the right of Indians to fish on the Nisqually and Puyallup Rivers.

The next year, six hundred Indian activists commanded nationwide attention by occupying a former prison on Alcatraz Island, located off the coast of San Francisco. The Indians demanded an Indian culture center on the island and used the media attention they were receiving to cite a long list of grievances over the treatment of Indians. Although the activists failed to accomplish their goal, they did keep their protest going for nineteen months, at the end of which time authorities forcibly removed them from Alcatraz. This protest, and many others, also helped to capture the attention of top government officials who were interested in addressing many wrongs done to Indians.

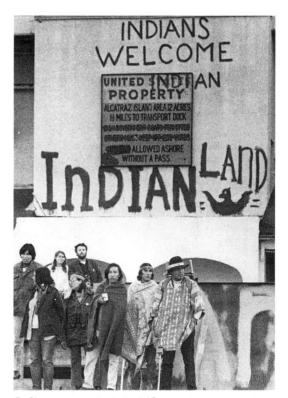

Indians stage a protest at Alcatraz to create publicity for their many grievances against the U.S. government.

Changes in Indian Policy

During the presidency of Lyndon Baines Johnson from 1963 to 1968, Native Americans witnessed the arrival of a new direction in Indian policy: a reemphasis on self-determination. Johnson proposed that the government help Indians achieve equality to whites in their standard of living and the freedom to reside on reservations or to move away. Indians, suggested Johnson, should become more involved in the making of decisions concerning their own lives.

But an even more historic shift in policy for Indians came in 1970 from the administration of the next president. Richard Nixon urged Congress to repeal the termination law completely and announced a policy that gave greater self-government to Native Americans, with the federal government helping to upgrade educational, legal, and medical services on reservations.

Taos Pueblo dancers perform in a celebration commemorating the return of Blue Lake in 1971.

Nixon pleased many Indians when he appointed Louis Bruce, a Native American, to head the BIA. Bruce made it his policy to fill the top job slots at the BIA with Native Americans whenever possible. Under Bruce the BIA changed substantially from an agency that managed Indians to one that served them.

The Nixon administration also broke with tradition when it convinced Congress to return Blue Lake and forty-eight thousand acres in New Mexico to the Taos Indian Pueblo. The return of this area, which was part of a sacred site taken improperly from the Indians in 1906, marked

the first time Indians ever received *lands* from the government, not money, in compensation for lost territories.

Wounded Knee 1973

The Nixon years were also marked by Indian anger and protest. On February 22, 1973, nearly three hundred armed Oglala Sioux, many of them members of the American Indian Movement (AIM) occupied the Pine Ridge Reservation at Wounded Knee, South Dakota—the site of the infamous massacre of 1890. Outraged by the recent killing of an Indian by a white in the nearby town of Custer, the protesters announced that they had "liberated" the village of Wounded Knee from white control. They also threatened violence unless Indian lands and rights were restored.

"Our message to the government was: 'Come and discuss our demands or kill us!'" recalls Mary Crow Dog, a Sioux participant in the Wounded Knee takeover.[124]

Soon, more than two hundred heavily armed FBI agents, U.S. marshals, and BIA police surrounded the town. A gun battle erupted between Indian militants and law enforcement officials, killing two people. Seventy-one days later, after peace negotiations, the Indians surrendered.

As a condition for peace, the government promised to investigate an 1868 treaty, which the Sioux felt the United States had violated. The government kept its word and ordered the required historical–legal research. It was found that the treaty was indeed valid, but the United States maintained that the treaty "was superseded by the U.S. power of 'eminent domain'— the government's power to take land."[125]

A militant AIM member protests at Wounded Knee in 1973. The protest ended in a gun battle between members of AIM and FBI agents.

Legal Struggles

Although budget concerns and various attempts to cut government waste have affected funding for Indian programs, official U.S. Indian policy has retained most of the historic changes introduced during the Nixon years.

Along with pushing for a change in government policy during this period, Indians waged legal struggles to seek hearings with respect to unsatisfactory treatment at the hands of governments and individuals in the past. Results of those efforts are mixed.

One of the most notable Indian victories had its roots in the Trade and Intercourse Act of 1790, which specified that no Indian lands could be taken without a treaty. The government, however, routinely ignored the treaty during the next century. Then in 1970 two Abenaki tribes, the Passamaquoddy and the Penobscot of Maine, won victories in the U.S. Supreme Court. A ruling that the Indians had been unlawfully deprived of their lands in 1790 included the welcome news that they were entitled to be compensated in the amount of $81.5 million.

The Wampanoag Indians of Mashpee, Massachusetts, however, lost a land claim suit to win back 13,700 acres on Cape Cod. A jury concluded in 1978 that the Wampanoag—who were among the first to greet the English more than 350 years ago—were no longer a tribe in 1870 when the disputed land was taken and therefore had no legal standing.

The Sioux were luckier in 1979 when they collected $100 million—the largest amount yet awarded an Indian group—for an area of land in the Black Hills taken from them in 1877. Later the Penobscot Indians in Maine won $481,580,000 in a legal settlement for illegal taking of the tribe's land in 1790. And on August 27, 1988, the Puyallup tribe won a $162 million settlement when it agreed to drop a lawsuit to reclaim property in Tacoma, Washington.

Altogether, Indians have also increased their tribal holdings since the 1930s, when allotment practices ceased. Today, tribes own about 96 million acres, or roughly 5 percent of all lands in the United States.

Despite these modest victories, though, big challenges remain for Native Americans today.

Confronting the Present

The days of flagrant land theft, wars, massacres, forced relocation, and termination are gone. But despite the changed atmosphere, many Native Americans believe they must remain vigilant to battle those who would deprive them of their lands.

A Sioux tribal chairman stands by a monument that marks the place where over one hundred Dakota were killed for allegedly participating in the Dakota Conflict over one hundred years ago.

In 1988, for example, a federal court enabled the U.S. Forestry Service to oust the Sioux from a section of the Black Hills—a clear violation, say Indian activists—of the Fort Laramie treaty of 1868. A state park and a recreational park were also established in Sioux territory in the Black Hills. In recent years, Congress ordered the Navajo in Arizona to vacate native lands to make way for exploration by mineral companies. On another occasion Navajo land was flooded by government authorities for a hydroelectric power project.

There are also disputes over land sites now clearly controlled by the federal government. Indians consider many of these to be sacred and use them for such purposes.

During the Reagan years, Secretary of the Interior James Watt gave permission for developers to make a ski resort on San Francisco peaks in Arizona—an area considered hallowed by the Navajo and Hopi.

Thus, in recent decades, Indians have learned that their cherished lands are not completely secure when the tribes are opposed by unrelenting pressure from big government and big business.

In fact, the federal government retains great authority over Indian land. For example, the power of eminent domain gives government the right to confiscate land from nearly anyone for public use, such as the construc-

A 1994 picture captures the dual identity of the Native American: suited in the traditional dress of his ancestors, this man is also a citizen of the government that forced the mass relocation of his people.

tion of a new airport or highway system. According to scholar Sharon O'Brien, "There is nothing . . . to prevent Congress from taking treaty held lands. Under domestic law, Congress has the authority to extinguish [nullify] recognized title and to abrogate [treat as nonexistent] Indian treaties."[126]

O'Brien also points out that Congress would have to compensate Indians for any loss of lands held under treaty. However, she adds, if a tribe has only aboriginal titles to the lands (that is, if the titles were never officially recognized by treaty or law), the government could confiscate the land without paying compensation.

Current Status of Native Americans

Experts estimate that when Columbus arrived in 1492, as many as a million Native Americans lived in what would become the United States. Their numbers had dipped to 300,000 by 1890, causing many observers to think that American Indians were well on the way to extinction.

Today, thanks to improved health care, better nutrition, and increasing birthrates, the number of North American Indians has bounced back; current estimates put the population between 1.5 and 2 million. According to the BIA, 503 distinct Native American communities exist in the United States and 278 reservations, where one-fourth of all American Indians now live. About half of all Indians live in the West, 27 percent in the South, 17 percent in the Midwest, and 0.6 percent in the Northeast. "The Myth of the Vanishing Redman, so strong in the literature, art, and social science of turn-of-the-century America, proved to be just that—a myth," argues historian Peter H. Wood.[127]

Thus, after five hundred years of repression and loss of native lands, North American Indians not only have survived, they have taken an active role in bettering their conditions. Currently, well-educated Indian activists and reformers are speaking out on behalf of Native Americans. Their goals include securing government aid to ease endemic economic and social problems, pressing various governments to honor existing treaties, preserving traditional culture and heritage, and taking greater command in the charting of their destinies.

As for the lost land of their ancestors? Most of it is irretrievably gone. And so too is much of an ancient way of life. Faced with this knowledge, many Native Americans must make an agonizing choice: to stay on tribal reservations and cling to a proud heritage or to leave and merge with the outside modern world.

Today, however, unlike the not-so-distant past, Indians may make this decision themselves.

Notes

Chapter 1: Whose Lands?

1. Little Rock Reed, "Broken Treaties, Broken Promises, The United States's Continuing Campaign Against Native People," May/June 1992, *SIRS 1992 History*, article 68. Boca Raton, FL: Social Issues Resources Series, 1992.

2. Quoted in Mary Ellen Jones, ed., *Christopher Columbus and His Legacy*. San Diego, CA: Greenhaven Press, 1992.

3. Peter H. Wood, "Re-Viewing the Map: America's 'Empty Wilderness,'" *SIRS 1992 Population*, Vol. 5, article 59. Boca Raton, FL: Social Issues Resources Series, 1992.

4. *The Log of Christopher Columbus*. Translated by Robert H. Fuson. Camden, ME: International Marine Publishing, 1987.

5. Quoted in *To America and Around the World: The Logs of Christopher Columbus and Ferdinand Magellan*. Translated by Clements S. Markham and John Pinkerton. Boston: Branden Publishing, 1990.

6. Quoted in Daniel Boorstin, *The Discoverers*. New York: Random House, 1983.

7. Quoted in Alistair Cooke, *America*. New York: Knopf, 1977.

8. Quoted in George W. Manypenny, *Our Indian Wards*. New York: Da Capo Press, 1972.

9. Quoted in Richard B. Morris and James Woodress, eds., *Voices from America's Past: Vol. 1, The Colonies and the New Nation*. New York: Dutton, 1961.

10. Quoted in Annette Rosenstiel, *Red & White: Indian Views of the White Man 1492–1982*. New York: Universe Books, 1983.

11. Quoted in Alan Axelrod, *Chronicle of the Indian Wars: From Colonial Times to Wounded Knee*. New York: Prentice Hall, 1993.

12. Quoted in Axelrod, *Chronicle of the Indian Wars*.

13. Quoted in Manypenny, *Our Indian Wards*.

14. Dee Brown, *Bury My Heart at Wounded Knee*. New York: Bantam, 1970.

15. Howard Zinn, *A People's History of the United States*. New York: Harper & Row, 1980.

16. Gary Wills, *Under God: Religion and American Politics*. New York: Simon and Schuster, 1990.

17. Quoted in Manypenny, *Our Indian Wards*.

18. Quoted in Morris and Woodress, *Voices from America's Past*.

19. Quoted in Jones, *Christopher Columbus and His Legacy*.

20. Janet A. McDonnell, *The Dispossession of the American Indian, 1887–1934*. Bloomington and Indianapolis: Indiana University Press, 1991.

21. Zinn, *A People's History of the United States*.

Chapter 2: Pushing the Indians West

22. Quoted in Wills, *Under God*.

23. Quoted in Daniel Boorstin, *The Americans: The Colonial Experience*. New York: Random House, 1958.

24. Quoted in Manypenny, *Our Indian Wards*.

25. Quoted in Christopher Davis, *North American Indian*. London: Hamlyn Publishing Group, 1969.

26. Quoted in Rosenstiel, *Red & White*.

27. Quoted in Rosenstiel, *Red & White*.

28. Oliver Perry Chitwood, *A History of Colonial America*. New York: Harper & Row, 1961.

29. Quoted in Axelrod, *Chronicle of the Indian Wars*.

30. Quoted in Peter Nabokov, ed., *Native American Testimony: An Anthology of Indian and White Relations, First Encounter to Dispossession*. New York Crowell, 1978.

31. Quoted in Edward S. Barnard, ed., *Story of the Great American West*. Pleasantville, NY: Reader's Digest, 1977.

32. Quoted in Manypenny, *Our Indian Wards*.

33. Quoted in Sanford Wexler, *Westward Expansion: An Eyewitness History*. New York: Facts On File, 1991.

34. Quoted in Henry Steele Commager, ed., *Documents of American History*. New York: Appleton-Century-Crofts, 1948.

35. Quoted in Axelrod, *Chronicle of the Indian Wars*.

36. Quoted in Wexler, *Westward Expansion*.

Chapter 3: Pushed to the Mississippi

37. Vine Deloria Jr., ed., *American Indian Policy in the Twentieth Century*. Norman and London: University of Oklahoma Press, 1985.

38. Robert William Mondy, *Pioneers and Preachers: Stories of the Old Frontier*. Chicago: Nelson-Hall, 1980.

39. Mondy, *Pioneers and Preachers*.

40. Quoted in Commager, *Documents of American History*.

41. Quoted in Davis, *North American Indian*.

42. Quoted in Wexler, *Westward Expansion*.

43. Quoted in Davis, *North American Indian*.

44. Quoted in Wexler, *Westward Expansion*.

45. Quoted in Davis, *North American Indian*.

46. Quoted in Rebecca Brooks Gruver, *An American History*, Vol. 1. Reading, MA: Addison-Wesley, 1972.

47. Quoted in Benjamin Capps, *The Indians*. New York: Time-Life Books, 1973.

48. Quoted in Wexler, *Westward Expansion*.

49. Quoted in Wexler, *Westward Expansion*.

50. Gruver, *An American History*.

51. Quoted in John M. Blum, William S. McFeely, Edmund S. Morgan, Arthur M. Schlesinger Jr., Kenneth M. Stampp, and C. Vann Woodward, *The National Experience: A History of the United States*, 6th ed. San Diego, CA: Harcourt Brace Jovanovich, 1985.

Chapter 4: Forced Removal Begins

52. Quoted in Manypenny, *Our Indian Wards*.

53. Quoted in Manypenny, *Our Indian Wards*.

54. Quoted in Robert V. Remini, *The Life of Andrew Jackson*. New York: Harper & Row, 1988.

55. Remini, *The Life of Andrew Jackson*.

56. Nabokov, *Native American Testimony*.

57. Quoted in Grant Foreman, *The Five Civilized Tribes*. Norman: University of Oklahoma Press, 1934.

58. Quoted in Commager, *Documents of American History*.

59. Quoted in Brown, *Bury My Heart at Wounded Knee*.

60. Brown, *Bury My Heart at Wounded Knee*.

61. Quoted in Wilfred T. Neill, *Florida's Seminole Indian*. St. Petersburg, FL: Great Outdoors, 1956.

62. Quoted in Neill, *Florida's Seminole Indian*.

63. Alexis de Tocqueville, *Democracy in America*. Translated by George Lawrence. New York: Harper & Row, 1988.

Chapter 5: The Disappearing Frontier

64. Quoted in Foreman, *The Five Civilized Tribes*.
65. Foreman, *The Five Civilized Tribes*.
66. Foreman, *The Five Civilized Tribes*.
67. Quoted in Wexler, *Westward Expansion*.
68. Brown, *Bury My Heart at Wounded Knee*.
69. Brown, *Bury My Heart at Wounded Knee*.
70. Quoted in Davis, *North American Indian*.
71. Ralph K. Andrist, *The Long Death: The Last Days of the Plains Indian*. New York: Macmillan, 1964.
72. Andrist, *The Long Death*.
73. Manypenny, *Our Indian Wards*.
74. Manypenny, *Our Indian Wards*.
75. Manypenny, *Our Indian Wards*.
76. Quoted in Andrist, *The Long Death*.

Chapter 6: Revolts, Removals, and Reservations

77. Quoted in Wexler, *Westward Expansion*.
78. Quoted in Brown, *Bury My Heart at Wounded Knee*.
79. Quoted in Brown, *Bury My Heart at Wounded Knee*.
80. Brown, *Bury My Heart at Wounded Knee*.
81. Irving Stone, *Men to Match My Mountains*. Garden City, NY: Doubleday, 1956.
82. Quoted in Stone, *Men to Match My Mountains*.
83. Quoted in Andrist, *The Long Death*.
84. Quoted in Andrist, *The Long Death*.
85. Quoted in Wexler, *Westward Expansion*.
86. Quoted in Andrist, *The Long Death*.
87. Quoted in Andrist, *The Long Death*.
88. Stone, *Men to Match My Mountains*.
89. Quoted in Capps, *The Indians*.
90. Quoted in Barnard, *Story of the Great American West*.

91. Quoted in Helen Hunt Jackson, *A Century of Dishonor (A Sketch of the United States Government's Dealings with Some of the Indian Tribes)*. Williamstown, MA: Corner House, 1973.
92. Quoted in Capps, *The Indians*.

Chapter 7: The Final Stand

93. S. L. A. Marshall, *Crimsoned Prairie: The Indian Wars on the Great Plains*. New York: Scribner's, 1972.
94. Quoted in Davis, *North American Indian*.
95. Quoted in Evan S. Connell, *Son of the Morning Star: Custer and the Little Bighorn*. San Francisco: North Point Press, 1984.
96. Quoted in Connell, *Son of the Morning Star*.
97. Quoted in Connell, *Son of the Morning Star*.
98. Quoted in Connell, *Son of the Morning Star*.
99. Quoted in Brown, *Bury My Heart at Wounded Knee*.
100. Rosenstiel, *Red & White*.
101. Quoted in Brown, *Bury My Heart at Wounded Knee*.
102. Quoted in Brown, *Bury My Heart at Wounded Knee*.
103. Quoted in Brown, *Bury My Heart at Wounded Knee*.
104. T. Roosevelt, "White Takeover of Indian Land: A White's View," in Jones, *Christopher Columbus and His Legacy*.
105. Quoted in Nabokov, *Native American Testimony*.

Chapter 8: Trying to Make Indians White

106. Quoted in Leonard Pitt, *We Americans, 1865 to the Present, Vol. II*. Glenview, IL:

Scott, Foresman, 1976.

107. Quoted in Davis, *North American Indian*.

108. Quoted in Nabokov, *Native American Testimony*.

109. Quoted in Frank W. Porter III, *The Bureau of Indian Affairs*. New York: Chelsea House, 1988.

110. Reed, "Broken Treaties, Broken Promises."

111. Quoted in Pitt, *We Americans*.

112. Quoted in McDonnell, *The Dispossession of the American Indian*.

113. McDonnell, *The Dispossession of the American Indian*.

114. Deloria, *American Indian Policy in the Twentieth Century*.

115. Quoted in McDonnell, *The Dispossession of the American Indian*.

Chapter 9: Forced into the Twentieth Century

116. McDonnell, *The Dispossession of the American Indian*.

117. Quoted in Donald Lee Fixico, *Termination and Relocation: Federal Indian Policy in the 1950s*. Norman: University of Oklahoma Press, 1980.

118. Quoted in Fixico, *Termination and Relocation*.

119. Fixico, *Termination and Relocation*.

120. Quoted in Fixico, *Termination and Relocation*.

121. Quoted in Sharon O'Brien, "Federal Indian Policies and Human Rights," in Deloria, *American Indian Policy in the Twentieth Century*.

122. Quoted in Porter, *The Bureau of Indian Affairs*.

123. Deloria, *American Indian Policy in the Twentieth Century*.

124. Mary Crow Dog, with Richard Erdoes, *Lakota Woman*. New York: Grove Weidenfeld, 1990.

125. Zinn, *A People's History of the United States*.

Epilogue: Confronting the Present

126. O'Brien, "Federal Indian Policies and Human Rights."

127. Wood, "Re-Viewing the Map."

For Further Reading

Daniel Boorstin, *The Discoverers*. New York: Random House, 1983. A popular history of how discoveries of the great explorers changed the world.

Arthur Diamond, *Smallpox and the American Indian*. San Diego, CA: Lucent Books, 1991. A compact yet concise and highly informative history of the impact of smallpox and other diseases on Native Americans.

Gordon Langley Hall, *Osceola*. New York: Holt, Rinehart and Winston, 1964. A widely researched and readable biography with many interesting excerpts from primary sources.

Lawrence C. Kelly, *Federal Indian Policy*. New York: Chelsea House, 1990. A readable history that gives a general overview of U.S. policy toward Native Americans from the colonial period to the present day.

Richard B. Morris, *The Indian Wars*. Minneapolis: Lerner, 1985. A concise and factual account for middle-school readers of the conflicts between Europeans and the Five Civilized Tribes along the Atlantic Coast.

Don Nardo, *The Indian Wars*. San Diego, CA: Lucent Books, 1991. A well-written, dramatic, and factual account of the major wars between European-Americans and Indians since the arrival of the English in North America.

Frank W. Porter III, *The Bureau of Indian Affairs*. New York: Chelsea House, 1988. A book for the general reader that traces the controversial history of the BIA from its beginning to its current status.

Russell Shorto, *Tecumseh, and the Dream of an American Indian Nation*. Englewood Cliffs, NJ: Silver Burdett, 1989. Informative and easy-to-read biography that traces the entire life of the great Shawnee leader. Scant use of primary sources in text.

John Upton Terrel, *Land Grab: The Truth About "The Winning of the West."* New York: Dial Press, 1972. An angry, highly subjective book clearly meant as an indictment against the United States for its dealings with the American Indians.

Jeanne Williams, *Trail of Tears: American Indians Driven from Their Lands*. Dallas, TX: Hendrik-Long, 1992. A dramatic narrative history, focusing on the forcible removal of the Comanche, Cheyenne, Apache, Navajo, and Cherokee from their ancient homelands.

Additional Works Consulted

To America and Around the World: The Logs of Christopher Columbus and Ferdinand Magellan. Translated by Clements S. Markham and John Pinkerton. Boston: Branden Publishing, 1990. (Columbus's logs transcribed by Las Casas; Magellan's logs written by Antonio Pigafetta.) A fascinating primary source containing translations of Columbus's initial reactions upon seeing the New World and its "Indians."

Ralph K. Andrist, *The Long Death: The Last Days of the Plains Indian.* New York: Macmillan, 1964. A scholarly but highly readable and interesting book.

Alan Axelrod, *Chronicle of the Indian Wars: From Colonial Times to Wounded Knee.* New York: Prentice Hall, 1993. A scholarly yet lively and informative retelling of the major Indian wars, enriched with insightful primary sources.

Edward S. Barnard, ed., *Story of the Great American West.* Pleasantville, NY: Reader's Digest, 1977. An entertaining popular history of the West for the general reader.

John M. Blum, William S. McFeely, Edmund S. Morgan, Arthur M. Schlesinger Jr., Kenneth M. Stampp, and C. Vann Woodward, *The National Experience: A History of the United States.* 6th ed. San Diego, CA: Harcourt Brace Jovanovich, 1985. A college-level textbook.

Daniel Boorstin, *The Americans: The Colonial Experience.* New York: Random House, 1958. A top-notch history of colonial days, with many primary accounts concerning relations between whites and Indians.

Dee Brown, *Bury My Heart at Wounded Knee.* New York: Bantam, 1970. This highly acclaimed and very readable book recounts, from the Indian point of view, how the West was lost.

Benjamin Capps, *The Indians.* New York: Time-Life Books, 1973. A comprehensive look at the culture and history of the Native Americans who inhabited the Old West, filled with a colorful array of drawings, pictures, and photos.

Oliver Perry Chitwood, *A History of Colonial America.* New York: Harper & Row, 1961. A scholarly work on America's colonial past.

Henry Steele Commager, ed., *Documents of American History.* New York: Appleton-Century-Crofts, 1948. A vast collection of documents that marked important stages in American history.

Evan S. Connell, *Son of the Morning Star: Custer and the Little Bighorn.* San Francisco: North Point Press, 1984. A readable yet highly detailed and lengthy biography of Custer.

Alistair Cooke, *America.* New York: Knopf, 1977. An entertaining, popular history for the general reader.

Mary Crow Dog, with Richard Erdoes, *Lakota Woman.* New York: Grove Weidenfeld, 1990. An intimate, first-person account for mature readers of a contemporary Indian woman growing up on a reservation in South Dakota.

Christopher Davis, *North American Indian.* London: Hamlyn Publishing Group, 1969. A lyrical, compressed narrative of the conquest of the American Indians and their struggle to exist in the modern world.

Vine Deloria Jr., ed., *American Indian Policy in the Twentieth Century.* Norman and London: University of Oklahoma Press, 1985. Eleven essays written by contemporary scholars, covering a wide range of federal Indian policies.

Executive Orders Relating to Indian Reservations, 1855–1922. Wilmington, DE: Scholarly Resources, 1975. A compilation, without commentary or narration, of the original orders pertaining to Indian reservations given by U.S. presidents and other government officials.

Eyewitnesses and Other Readings in American History, Vol. 2: 1865 to the Present. Austin, TX: Holt, Rinehart and Winston, 1991. A compilation of primary sources.

Donald Lee Fixico, *Termination and Relocation: Federal Indian Policy in the 1950s.* Norman: University of Oklahoma Press, 1980. A scholarly yet readable doctoral dissertation. Numerous quotes from government sources.

Grant Foreman, *The Five Civilized Tribes.* Norman, University of Oklahoma Press, 1934. A detailed, scholarly book that relies on missionary letters, government documents, and interviews with survivors of forced relocation.

Thomas Froncek, ed., *Voices from the Wilderness.* New York: McGraw-Hill, 1974. A compilation of personal accounts of America's frontiersmen in their own words, from 1775 to 1870.

Geronimo, *Geronimo: His Own Story.* Edited by S.M. Barrett. Newly edited with an introduction and notes by Frederick W. Turner III. New York: Ballantine, 1970. A very readable and updated translated version of the Apache warrior's orally transmitted autobiography.

Rebecca Brooks Gruver, *An American History.* Vol. 1. Reading, MA: Addison-Wesley, 1972. A college-level textbook on American history until 1877.

Helen Hunt Jackson, *A Century of Dishonor (A Sketch of the United States Government's Dealings with Some of the Indian Tribes).* Williamstown, MA: Corner House, 1973. A classic documentary, which originally appeared in 1881. This dramatic indictment of U.S. Indian policy, based heavily on government documents, helped arouse the American conscience.

Mary Ellen Jones, ed., *Christopher Columbus and His Legacy*. San Diego, CA: Greenhaven Press, 1992. A compilation of widely diverse writings, ranging over hundreds of years, which deal with the impact of Columbus's discovery on Indians.

Richard M. Ketchum, ed., *The American Heritage Book of the Pioneer Spirit*. New York: American Heritage, 1959. A popular history, interesting for its omissions concerning the dispossession of Indians.

Arleen Keylin and Eve Nelson, eds., *If Elected*. New York: Random House, 1976. A compilation of authentic *New York Times* front-page news reports from 1860 to 1960.

The Log of Christopher Columbus. Translated by Robert H. Fuson. Camden, ME: International Marine Publishing, 1987. A translated version of Columbus's log, enhanced by a fascinating blend of maps, illustrations, and engravings.

Janet A. McDonnell, *The Dispossession of the American Indian, 1887–1934*. Bloomington and Indianapolis: Indiana University Press, 1991. A concise, scholarly book, which traces the disastrous impact on Indians of the federal government's forty-seven-year allotment policy.

Thomas E. Mails, *The Cherokee People: The Story of the Cherokees from Earliest Origins to Contemporary Times*. Tulsa, OK: Council Oak Books, 1992. A comprehensive, scholarly yet readable and richly illustrated book that traces the origin and history of the Cherokee people.

George W. Manypenny, *Our Indian Wards*. New York: Da Capo Press, 1972. A classic work, which first appeared in 1880. The author was commissioner of Indian Affairs from 1853 to 1857, and he drew on personal experiences to plead for Indian reform.

S. L. A. Marshall, *Crimsoned Prairie: The Indian Wars on the Great Plains*. New York: Scribner's, 1972. Written by a military historian, this work focuses on the battlefield tactics of the Indian wars.

Robert William Mondy, *Pioneers and Preachers: Stories of the Old Frontier*. Chicago: Nelson-Hall, 1980. An interesting, readable, and well-documented account of everyday existence on America's early frontiers.

Richard B. Morris and James Woodress, eds., *Voices from America's Past: Vol. I, The Colonies and the New Nation*. New York: Dutton, 1961. A collection of eyewitness accounts of America's colonial period.

Peter Nabokov, ed., *Native American Testimony: An Anthology of Indian and White Relations, First Encounter to Dispossession*. New York: Crowell, 1978. A fascinating collection of readable primary sources, in the voices of American Indians, which convey the story of Indian and white encounters in America.

Wilfred T. Neill, *Florida's Seminole Indian.* St. Petersburg, FL: Great Outdoors, 1956. A concise, readable history of the Seminoles for the general reader.

Leonard Pitt, *We Americans, Vol. II, 1865 to the Present.* Glenview, IL: Scott, Foresman, 1976. A college-level textbook.

Little Rock Reed, "Broken Treaties, Broken Promises, The United States's Continuing Campaign Against Native People," May/June 1992, *SIRS 1992 History*, article 68. Boca Raton, FL: Social Issues Resources Series, 1992.

Robert V. Remini, *The Life of Andrew Jackson.* New York: Harper & Row, 1988. A condensation of a three-volume work by a renowned historian. Highly readable. More sympathetic to Jackson than other writers.

Annette Rosenstiel, *Red & White: Indian Views of the White Man 1492–1982.* New York: Universe Books, 1983. A fascinating collection of primary sources tracing the Indians' view of their own removal and destruction over five centuries.

Irving Stone, *Men to Match My Mountains.* Garden City, NY: Doubleday, 1956. An epic retelling of the opening of the Far West, mainly from the white race's point of view.

Alexis de Tocqueville, *Democracy in America.* Translated by George Lawrence. New York: Harper & Row, 1988. This classic work, written by a French observer, contains thought-provoking, firsthand descriptions of the condition of the American Indians in early-nineteenth-century America.

Sanford Wexler, *Westward Expansion: An Eyewitness History.* New York: Facts On File, 1991. A very readable narrative and fascinating compilation of primary sources, expressing a wide range of views of those who witnessed the westward expansion, victors and victims alike.

Gary Wills, *Under God: Religion and American Politics.* New York: Simon and Schuster, 1990. A book for the mature and serious reader, concerning the mingling of religion and politics in American history.

Peter H. Wood, "Re-Viewing the Map: America's 'Empty Wilderness,'" *SIRS 1992 Population,* Vol. 5, article 59. Boca Raton, FL: Social Issues Resources Series, 1992.

Howard Zinn, *A People's History of the United States.* New York: Harper & Row, 1980. This popular history for the general reader relies heavily on primary sources and quotations from those who have been exploited throughout the history of the United States.

Index

Abenakis, 14, 29, 111
Acadia, 27, 28
Alabama, 44, 47
Alcatraz occupation, 109
alcohol
    disastrous effect of, 24
Alexander IV, Pope
    land grants and, 11
Algonquins, 14, 30
allotment, 96-99, 103
American Indian Movement (AIM), 110
American Revolution, 33-35
The Americans: The Colonial Experience (Boorstin), 27
Andrist, Ralph K., 65, 67
annuities, 93
Anthony, Major Scott J., 75
Apaches, 72
Appalachian Mountains
    as boundary of colonial expansion, 27
    proclamation line and, 31
Arapahos, 64, 74, 78
    resistance of non-treaty bands of, 79-80
Arikaras, 64
Arizona, 63
Arkansas, 54
Armstrong, Francis W., 59
assimilation, 94-95, 105-106
Assiniboines, 64
Atsinas, 64
attitudes
    of French settlers, 13
    of Jamestown colonists, 14-15
    of western Americans, 64

Barboncito, 72
Barnard, Edward S., 83
Barrett, S.M., 9
Battle of Horseshoe Bend, 44
Battle of Little Big Horn, 82-83
Beveridge, Albert, 95
Bible, 17
Big Foot, 89
Blackfeet, 107
Black Hawk, 55-56
Black Hawk War, 56
Black Hills, 78, 81-82
Black Kettle, 75, 80
Blue Lake, 110
Board of Indian Commissioners, 94

Boorstin, Daniel, 27
Bosque Redondo, 72-74
Bozeman Trail, 77
Brazil, 11
Brown, Dee, 17, 54, 62, 63, 73, 74
Buffalo Bird Woman, 91
Bureau of Indian Affairs (BIA)
    call for abolition of, 105
    call for reform of, 109
    corruption in , 93
    creation of, 92
    selloff of lands and, 101
Bury My Heart at Wounded Knee (Brown), 74
Butler, Elizur, 52

Caddoes, 59
Canada, 27, 29, 35, 43
cannibalism, 12
Carleton, General James, 72
Carlisle Indian School, 95
Carson, Kit, 73
Catholic Church, 11
    official policy of, 12
A Century of Dishonor (Jackson), 93, 94
Chandler, O.K., 105
Cherokee Nation v. Georgia, 51
The Cherokee People (Mail), 55
Cherokees, 8, 32, 45, 46
    resistance to Indian Removal Act, 51-52
    Trail of Tears and, 52-53
Cheyenne, 64, 78
    resistance of non-treaty bands of, 79-80
    Sand Creek massacre of, 74-76
Chickasaws, 45, 46, 51, 59
Chief Joseph, 85-86
children
    raising of, 9
Chippewas, 30, 31, 38
Chitwood, Oliver Perry, 26
Chivington, John, 75, 77
Choctaws, 45, 46, 59
    forced removal of, 49-51
Christianity, 17
church aid, 59-60
citizenship, 105
Civil War, 72
    opportunities for Indians during, 69
Collier, John, reform of Indian Affairs and, 103-104

Colorado, massacres in , 74-76
Columbus, Christopher, 12, 113
    land claims of, 10-11
Comanches, 65, 78, 81, 86
Congress, U.S., 37, 42, 59
Connecticut, 19
conquistadors, 12-13
Continental Congress, 34
Cooke, Alistair, 11
Coville Reservation, 86
Crazy Horse, 84, 85
Creeks, 8, 44, 45, 46, 59
    forced removal of, 53
Crimsoned Prairie (Marshall), 81
Crook, General George, 81
Crow Dog, Mary, 110
Crows, 64
culture
    loss of Indian, 24, 94-95, 106
    struggle between white and Indian, 9
Curtis, Major General Samuel R., 75
Custer, Colonel George Armstrong
    defeat of, 82-84
    discovery of Black Hills gold by, 81
    Washita River massacre and, 80

Dakota Territory, 71
Darwin, Charles, 95-96
Dawes Severalty Act, 96-99, 103
Declaration of Indian Purpose, 109
Delawares, 26, 28, 30, 34-35, 59, 66
Deloria, Vine, Jr., 35
    allotments and, 99
    termination policy and, 108
Democracy in America (de Tocqueville), 50
Denmark, 13
devils
    European view of Indians as, 12, 17
discovery
    right of, 20
diseases
    effect on Indians of, 24, 59
The Dispossession of the American Indian (McDonnell), 97
Doddridge, Rev. Joseph, 27
Dog Soldiers, 75
Douglas, Stephen A., 66
Dreamer Religion, 87-88
Dunmore, Lord, 33

education, 95

Eisenhower, Dwight D.
    initiation of termination policy by,
        108
elders
    role of, 9
England, 29, 31
    colonization by, 14-17
    conflict with colonists, 31-33
    containment of U.S. by, 43
    French rivalry with, 14, 27-29
    right of discovery by, 20
English forces, 38
enslavement
    of Indians, 18-20
Europeans
    attitudes toward Indians, 10-11, 17,
        20-22, 23-25
Evans, John, 74
Everglades, 57

Fallen Timbers, 38
farming
    as only right use of land, 21, 25
    Dawes Act and, 96-99
    Indian attitudes toward, 97-98
federal government, 73, 85
    acquisition of Indian land, 66
    authority in Indian affairs, 48,
        114-115
    Indian land ownership by, 35
    management of Indian Territory
        and, 59-60
    peace commissions, 78
Fetterman, Captain William J., 77
Fitzgerald, Thomas, 68
Five Civilized Tribes, 46-47, 59-60, 67,
    79, 100
The Five Civilized Tribes (Foreman)
    67
Fixico, Donald Lee, 106
Florida, 13, 29, 35, 41, 56-57
forced removal. See removal, forced
Foreman, Grant, 59
Forestry Service, U.S., 112
Fort Atkinson agreements, 65
Fort Detroit, 30
Fort Duquesne, 29
Fort Hill Tower, 19
Fort Laramie, 74
    Conference, 64-65, 69
Fort Sill, 81
Fort Stanwyx, 31
Fox, 55, 66
France
    colonization by, 13-14
    English rivalry with, 14, 27-29
    sale of Louisiana by, 39
    treatment of Indians by, 13-14
Franklin, Benjamin, 24

Frelinghuysen, Theodore
    on protest against Indian Removal
        Act, 48
French and Indian War, 28-29, 35

Gallatin, Albert, 45
General Allotment Act, 96-99, 103
George, king of England, 34
Georgia, 20, 27, 31, 47
    forced removal of Cherokees in,
        51-53
Geronimo, 87
Ghost Dance, 87-88
gold
    discovery of
        in Black Hills, 81
        in California, 63-64
        in Cherokee lands, 48
        in Montana and Wyoming, 76
Grant, Ulysses S., 84
Grattan, John L., 69
Great Lakes, 29, 31, 41
Great Plains, 62, 65
Great Spirit, 9, 22, 29, 30, 88, 107
Grundy, Felix, 43
Gruver, Rebecca Brooks, 44

Hard Labor treaty, 32
Harrison, William Henry, 40-42
Hazen, General, 80
Hidatsas, 91
A History of Colonial America
    (Chitwood), 26
Holland, 13, 26
Hoover Commission, 105
Hopis, 8
House Concurrent Resolution, 107-
    108
human sacrifice, 12
Hurons, 14
Hutchinson, Thomas
    on the Indian plague, 24

Illinois, 37, 55
Indiana, 37
Indian Claims Commission, 107
Indian Removal Act, 48-49, 57
Indian Reorganization Act of 1934,
    103-104
Indians
    European diseases and, 24
    reasons for European defeat of,
        23-25
Indian Territory
    incorporated into United States,
        100
    suffering in, 59
    westward migration and, 62-63
Iowas, 66

Iroquois, 34
Jackson, Andrew
    Black Hawk War and, 55-56
    Cherokee removal and, 52
    defeat of Creeks by, 44
    Indian Removal Act and, 47-49
    legacy of, 58
    Seminole resistance and, 56-57
Jackson, Helen Hunt, 93
James, king of England, 14
Jamestown colony, 14-16
Jefferson, Thomas
    contradictory views of, 38-39
    Louisiana Purchase by, 39-40
Johnson, Lyndon B., 109-110
Johnson, William, 32-33
joint-stock company, 14
Joseph, chief of Nez Percé, 85-86

Kansas, 66-67
Kansas City, 54
Kaskaskias, 66
Keechies, 59
Kentucky, 31
Kickapoos, 59, 66
King George, 34
King James, 14
King Philip, 19
King Powhatan. See Wahunsonacock
Kiowas, 65, 78, 81, 86
Klamaths, 87

Lake Erie, 43
Lake Michigan, 43
Lakota Woman (Crow Dog), 112
Lancaster
    attack on, 19
land
    attitudes about
        American, 31-33, 35
        European, 13, 17, 20-22
        Indian, 17, 107
    boundaries of, 22, 35
    claims to, 10, 20
    confiscation of, 47, 101
    Dawes Act and allotments of, 96-99
    insecurity of present, 112
    ownership of, 21-22
    Proclamation of 1763 and, 31-33
    sale of, 100-102
    Spanish titles to, 12
    theft of, 68
    treaty diminishment of, 66, 74, 78
Land Ordinance of 1785, 37
land warrants, 31
La Salle, 13
lawsuits, 111
Lean Bear, 75
Leavenworth, 68

legal contracts
conflict over, 17, 22
Le Loutre, Abbé Jean-Louis, 27-28
Leupp, Francis, 96
"life, liberty, and property," 22
Lincoln, Abraham, 71
line of demarcation, 11, 13
Little Crow, 71
Little Rock Reed, 10
Little Turtle, 38, 41
Lochaber treaty, 32
Locke, John 21-22
Lone Wolf, 100
The Long Death (Andrist), 65
Louisiana, 54
Louisiana Purchase, 39
Louisiana Territory, 39-40
Louis the Great, 13
Low Dog, 83

McDonnell, Janet A., 22, 97, 103
McKinley, William, 100
Mail, Thomas E., 55
Maine, 27, 31
Major Crimes Act of 1885, 97
Manifest Destiny, 60-61
Manypenny, George W., 17, 68
on encroachment of Indian lands,
67
Marshall, Chief Justice John
Cherokee case and, 51-52
on right of discovery, 11
Marshall, S.L.A., 81
Massachusetts Bay Colony, 16-19
Mather, Cotton, 18, 24
Medicine Lodge Creek, 78
Menominees, 108
Mescaleros, 72
Metacomet, 18
Mexican War, 63
Miamis, 38, 66
Michigan, 30, 37
Miles, Colonel Nelson, 86
Minnesota, 66
Minnesota River Valley, 71
Mississippi, 47
Mississippi River
as boundary of French claims, 29
as boundary of Indian Territory,
54
as boundary of United States, 35
French expansion along, 13
Monroe and removal of tribes
beyond, 46-47
United States acquisition of, 39
Mississippi Valley
English land grants in, 29
Missouri, 54, 62
Missourias, 66

Modocs, 81
Mohegans, 19
Mondy, Robert William, 35-37
Monroe, James, 46
Mormons, 62
Morrill, Lot M., 78
Myrick, Andrew, 70-71

Nabokov, Peter, 18, 49, 86
Narragansets, 19
*The National Experience: A History of the
United States* (Blum), 52
National Indian Youth Council (NIYC),
109
Native American Testimony (Nabokov),
18, 49, 86
Navajos
development in lands of, 112
forced removal of, 72-73
Nebraska, 66-67
New England
Indian plague in, 24
New Jersey, 31
New Mexico, 63, 72
New York Morning News, 61
Nez Percé
forced removal of the, 85-86
Nipmucs, 19
Nixon, Richard, 110
nomadic peoples
end of way of life as, 94
right of occupancy and, 21
non-treaty bands
resistance of, 79-80
Northwest Ordinance of 1787,
37-38
Northwest Territory, 30-31, 37, 39-45
Norton, A.B., 74
Nova Scotia, 27

O'Brien, Sharon, 115
occupancy
right of, 13, 20, 21, 35
Ohio, 37
Ohio Company, 29
Ohio River
as boundary of Northwest Territory,
37
as proposed boundary for Indian
lands, 32
Ohio Valley, 27, 28, 31
Oklahoma, 53, 67
land seizure, 99-100
Omahas, 66
Openchancanough, 16
Oregon, 62, 81, 87
Oregon Trail, 62, 64, 65
Osceola, 57
O'Sullivan, John Louis, 61

Ottawas, 29-30, 31
Ottoes, 66
Paiutes, 87
Parker, Quannah, 86
Passamaquoddys, 111
Peace Commission, 77-79
Pennsylvania, 26, 31
Penn, William
honesty of, 26
on Indians and liquor, 25
Penobscots, 111
Peorias, 66
Pequots, 19
slaughter of, 18
Piankashaws, 66
Pilgrims, 16
Pine Ridge Reservation occupation,
110
*Pioneers and Preachers: Stories of the Old
Frontier* (Mondy), 35-37
Pittsburgh, 29, 35
Plymouth Rock, 16
Pontiac, 29-31
Pontiac's Rebellion, 30
population
European colonial, 23, 27
increase in U.S., 60
Indian, 115
land sales and growth in, 103
Ohio Valley, 38
Portugal
line of demarcation and, 11
Potawatamis, 30, 31, 38
Powder River massacre, 76
Powhatans
Jamestown colony and, 14-16
Proclamation of 1763, 31-33, 35
Prophet's Town, 42
Puritans, 16-19
Puyallups, 112

Quebec, 13

racism, 95-96
railroads, 66, 78
Rain-in-the-Face, 84
Ramona (Jackson), 94
*Red & White: Indian Views of the White
Man 1492-1982* (Rosenstiel), 88
Red Cloud, 76
Red Dog, 93
Reed, Little Rock, 95
religion
Dreamer, 87-88
end of ban on Indian, 104
Indian policy and, 17, 21
Manifest Destiny and, 61
undermining of Indian, 94-95
Remini, Robert V., 48-49

removal, forced, 46-47
of Choctaws, 49-51
of Creeks, 53
of Navajos, 72-73
of Seminoles, 56-57
of the Nez Percé, 85-86
reservations
first plan for, 16
system of, 92-93
termination of, 108
Rhode Island, 26
right of discovery, 20
right of occupancy, 13, 20, 21, 35
rights
loss of treaty, 93
of Indians, 31, 39
to use violence to take lands, 17
Rio Grande, 63, 72
Roosevelt, Franklin D., 103
Roosevelt, Theodore, 10, 90
Rosenstiel, Annette, 88
Rowlandson, Mary, 19
Royal Navy, 43
Russia, 13

Sac, 55, 66
Samoset, 17
Santa Fe Trail, 65
Schwabe, George, 105
Sells, Cato, 101
Seminoles, 45, 46, 59
resistance and forced removal of,
56-57
severalty. *See* Dawes Severalty Act
Shawnees, 30, 31, 38, 59, 66
Sheridan, General Philip, 92
Sherman, William Tecumseh, 80
Shingas, 28
Sibley, Colonel Henry Hastings, 71
Sioux, 64
AIM and, 110
attack at Powder River, 77
beginning of wars with, 69-70
Black Hills compensation for, 112
relocation to Black Hills, 79
resistance to white settlement, 81-82
victory at Battle of Little Big Horn,
83-84
Wounded Knee massacre of, 89
Sitting Bull, 84, 87, 88
slavery
debate on, 66
smallpox, 24
Smith, Captain John, 14-15, 18
Smith, James, 36
Smolalla, 87
Snyder Act, 105

social Darwinism, 95-96
Society of Friends (Quakers), 48
Spain, 26, 29, 57
line of demarcation and, 11
New World empire of, 12-13
Stone, Irving, 75, 76
Story of the Great American West
(Barnard), 83
Supreme Court, U.S., 100

Tammany, 26
Taos Pueblo, 110
Tecumseh
alliance with England of, 43
confederacy organized by, 41-42
death of, 44
qualities of, 41
Tenskwatawa, 42
termination, 106-108
*Termination and Relocation: Federal Indian
Policy in the 1950s* (Fixico), 106
territorial expansion, 43
Texas
settlement of, 62-63
Tippecanoe Creek, 42
Tocqueville, Alexis de, 50, 58
trade
English intention to, 14
Franch settlers and fur, 13
Trail of Tears, 52-53
treaties, 34-35
between Cherokees and the United
States, 51
Fort Laramie, 64-65
government violation of, 93
walking and riding, 22
Treaty of Camp Moultrie, 57
Treaty of Dancing Rabbit Creek, 49
Treaty of Greenville, 38
Treaty of Paris, 29
tribal corporations, 104
United Colonies, 16
Utah Territory, 62
Utes, 86

Van Buren, Martin, 52
von Vattel, Emmerich, 21
Virginia, 31, 33
Virginia Colony, 14, 17
Voices from the Wilderness (Froncek), 36

Wahunsonacock, 15
warning to settlers by, 18
Wampanoags, 17, 18-19, 111
Wanapums, 87
war
among tribes, 8

between English and Indians, 18-20
European advantage in, 23
Indian methods of, 36
with Powhatans, 15-16
War of 1812, 42-45
effect on Indians of, 44
support for, 43
War of Independence, 33-35
Washington, George
as "Town Destroyer," 34
defeat of French by, 29
war against Little Turtle and, 38
Washington Treaty, 53
Washita River massacre, 80
Watt, James, 114
Wayne, General Anthony, 38
weapons
European superiority in, 23
Weas, 66
Webster, Captain L.B., 55
West Indies, 19
West Virginia, 32
Westward Expansion: An Eyewitness History
(Wexler), 42, 77
Wexler, Sanford, 42, 77
Whipple, Rev. H.B., 71, 78
White Antelope, 75
Williams, Roger, 25-26
Wills, Gary
on fear of Indians as devils, 17
Winnebagos, 71
Winning of the West (Roosevelt), 90
Winthrop, John, 17
Wirt, William, 51
Wisconsin, 37
Wood, Peter H., 115
on underestimation of Indian
population, 10
Worcester, Samuel, 52
Worcester v. Georgia, 52
World War I, 102
World War II, effect on Indians, 104-
105
Wounded Knee
massacre, 89
takeover by AIM, 110-111
Wovoka, 87
Wyandots, 30
Wyatt, Francis, 16
Wyoming, 64

Zinn, Howard, 17
on brutality of English colonization,
22
Zunis, 8

Picture Credits

About the Author

John M. Dunn is a freelance writer and high school history teacher. He has taught in Georgia, Florida, North Carolina, and Germany. As a writer and journalist, he has published over 250 articles and stories in more than 20 periodicals, as well as scripts for audiovisual productions and a children's play. His book *The Russian Revolution* was published by Lucent Books in 1993. He lives with his wife and two daughters in Ocala, Florida.